© 2018 Liz M. Weiman. iWorkshop Academy Press
All rights reserved. Printed in the United States of America.
100+ iPhone/iPad Tricks You Can Do Right Now! (iOS 12 edition)

13-digit   ISBN 978-0-9961793-5-5

Contents

CHAPTER 1
Time-Saving Tricks   3

CHAPTER 5
New Texting App Tricks   41

CHAPTER 6
Additional Updates to Apple Apps   57

CHAPTER 7
Additional App Updates   79

CHAPTER 8
iOS 12 Key Updates & Tricks   95

APPENDIX A
Passcode, Touch ID, and Face ID Settings   113

APPENDIX B
Online Courses From iWorkshop Academy   117

About the Author

Liz M. Weiman has trained thousands of individuals since the early 1990s in computer/digital software, and has additionally created Web-content, e-learning modules, and instructional/technical documentation for Hewlett-Packard, Schlumberger, and other Fortune 500 companies. Ms. Weiman is also the author of "The Lawyer's Guide to Concordance", published by the American Bar Association, and "80+ iPhone/iPad Tricks You Can Do Right Now (iOS 11)."

In addition, she has been an instructor in Macintosh, iPad, iPhone, Apple Watch, and PC systems at The Women's Institute of Houston for the past 15 years. A Houston, Texas native who graduated from Boston University, she served as a fiction reviewer for the Houston Chronicle and other national newspapers, and as senior editor of Southwest Art Magazine. She has worked as a journalist, editor, instructional designer, technical writer, and documentation project manager.

Introduction

The term "iOS" stands for Apple's operating system. An operating system (OS) is the main software that takes care of the underlying processes that run your iPhone/iPad and/or computer, and there are typically seven or more updates available for your devices per year. A version number is given to all new major updates (e.g. iOS **12**), however smaller updates (mostly fixes) are added after a major update (e.g. iOS **12.1.2**). These updates typically usher in changes to many of the apps we use regularly.

I decided to create this guide due to the ever-changing iOS landscape, and because my students asked me to help them navigate the often-confusing changes brought about by continual updates. To this end, I have included 100+ tricks as individual "recipes," each accompanied by detailed instructions and background information, so users can perform the steps, while understanding the context of how each trick can be of benefit in the larger scope of their devices.

We will cover a plethora of new iOS 12 features, including the exciting **Measure** app, additional **Control Center** tiles, **AirDrop Password sharing**, **group FaceTime video calls, Siri Shortcuts, group Notifications, iMessage photo texting with effects, shapes, and filters**, and much more. We will also revisit little-known or forgotten tricks from earlier upgrades such as **scanning legal-sized documents** on the fly into the **Notes** app, **shaking** the phone to restore deletions, **turning Web pages and documents** into **PDFs**, and other tricks meant to save time and enhance daily productivity. Using these tricks, formerly time-consuming tasks can be accomplished in a matter of minutes, and users can become more fully empowered.

Note: Before beginning, please go to the section at the end of this guide titled "**Lingo to Know**" in order to review the glossary of terms and their definitions that are used throughout this guide (e.g. terms such as **apps**, **iOS**, **widgets**, etc.). Also take a look at Appendix C, where there is a list of important shortcuts to know about for iPads, iPhone models 10/X, XS/Max, XR, 8, 8 Plus, and earlier.

100+ iPhone/iPad Tricks You Can Do Right Now!

Before beginning the tricks, make sure to check which version of Apple's operating system is installed on your device.

1. From the **Home** screen, tap the **Settings** app, tap **General**, and then tap **About**.

2. Scroll down until you see **Version**. Your current iOS version number displays.

To upgrade your version to the latest iOS 12.x update:

1. From the **Home** screen, tap the **Settings** app, tap **General**, and then tap **Software Update**.

2. The screen will display **Checking for Updates**. After a few seconds, you will either be informed that you have the most current version or you will be prompted to **Download and Install** the latest version. If you plan to upgrade, make sure your device is plugged into an outlet, and then follow the on-screen instructions to complete the update.

Time-Saving Tricks

1

 ## Trick 1:

Turn Your iPhone into a Magnifying Glass

It's time to get out your device(s) and begin! Let's start with the first trick which comes in very handy when you don't have a magnifying glass nearby.

Note: In the last iOS update (11.x), the **Magnifier** was added to the list of "controls" or "tiles" (icons) that you could add to **Control Center**. See **Chapter 2** for how to add the **Magnifier** control to **Control Center** to access this feature in the future.

1. From the **Home** screen, tap the **Settings** app, tap **General**, and then tap **Accessibility**.

2. Tap **Magnifier**, and then slide the white circle to the right to enable (turn on) this feature.

After you have enabled this setting, you can press the **Home** button **three times in succession** (or **press the O n/O ff button** on the iPhone 10/X, XS/Max, XR models three times in succession) in order to turn your phone into a temporary magnifying glass.

Figure 1.1: Magnifier tools

When launched, the **Magnifier** displays several tools as follows:

- ☐ **Magnification slider to Zoom In and Out**

- ☐ **Focus Lock**

- ☐ **Freeze Frame**

- ☐ **Flashlight**

- ☐ **Color Filters** (which lead to a second screen of tools)

Note: See **Chapter 7** for more **Magnifier** tricks, and see **Chapter 8** to learn about the new **Measure** app and the **Level** tool, which turn your device into a "tape measure" and level respectively!

To turn off the **Magnifier**, tap **Home** (or **Off/On** on some models).

Congratulations! You have completed your first trick. Next, we will look at the **Lock** screen, which has many handy features

Lock Screen Tricks

Understanding the **Lock**, **Passcode**, and **Home** screens is integral to taking advantage of many of the new features in the latest operating system upgrade, and for working with some of the upcoming tricks. As such, a short explanation of these screens precedes the rest of the tricks in this chapter.

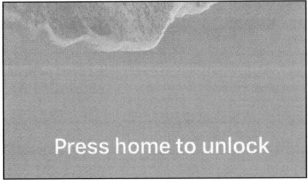

Figure 1.2: Lock screen (in models earlier than iPhone X models)

The Lock Screen

When you turn on (or wake up) your iPhone/iPad, the first screen that you encounter is called the **Lock** screen (see Figure 1.2). At the bottom of the screen, you may see the **Press home to unlock** message (unless you have the iPhone X models which unlock your device using **Face ID)**.

> **Note:** For more information about setting up **Face ID, Touch ID**, and your **Passcode**, see **Appendix A** in this book.

Figure 1.3: Passcode screen: Touch ID   Figure 1.4: X models screen

The Passcode Screen

When you press the **Home** button at the **Lock** screen (or **swipe up from the base** on the iPhone X models), a keypad may display a message that reads **Touch ID or Enter Passcode** (Figure 1.3) or **Enter Passcode** (Figure 1.4). This message means that you must type in your **passcode** or – on models supporting **Touch ID** – press your finger on the **Home** button so that your fingerprint can be read in order to use your device(s).

> **Note: Touch ID** is only available in certain models earlier than the iPhone X models and must be set up first in order for your fingerprint to be read. On the iPhone X, XS/Max, and XR models, you can also set up **Face ID** to unlock your device. For information about setting up **Touch ID** or **Face ID**, see **Appendix A** in this book.

If you have not encountered the **Passcode** screen, it could be that you have never set up a **passcode**. Operating without a **Lock** screen can make your phone more vulnerable to being stolen and/or hacked. If this occurs, your email contacts could be infiltrated, your identity stolen, and more. To learn how to set up a **passcode**, **Touch ID**, or **Face ID,** see the steps in **Appendix A** at the end of this book.

Lock and Unlock Your iPhone/iPad

You can lock your iPhone/iPad screen at any time by pressing, and then letting go of, the **On/Off** button found at the right side (or top) of your device. For instance, you might want to lock your phone when you are not using it, instead of waiting for the device to go to sleep automatically (a process called **auto-lock**). Here is how to lock and unlock your device:

❑   To lock your screen, press and then let go of the **On/Off** button on your iPhone/iPad at the right side (or top) of your device.

❑   To wake your phone, press the **On/Off** button again. On devices other than the iPhone X models, you will see the "**Press Home to unlock**" message at the **Lock** screen. For the iPhone X models, you can wake your device by tapping the screen or **swiping up from the base**. On some models, your device can wake without pressing a button or swiping. Instead, you can simply change a setting in the **Settings** app, as shown in **Trick 5**.

❑   In iOS 12, you can add security features to your **Lock** screen. For instance, hackers can access your iPhone/iPad using a USB connection to download data from your device(s). To prevent this, you can check this feature by tapping **Settings** > **Touch ID** (or **Face ID**) **& Passcode**. After you enter your passcode, you can scroll to the bottom to make sure the **USB Accessories** choice is off.

 # Trick 2:

Bypass the Passcode Screen With Your Fingerprint (iPad/iPhone 8/8 Plus & earlier models only)

On select iPhone models you can set up a feature that allows you to bypass the **passcode** screen by using your fingerprint. Once this feature is enabled, you can bypass the **Passcode** screen, and access your device by simply resting your finger on the **Home** button.

Note: In models that support **Touch ID**, you must enroll your fingerprint in your device before setting this up. For more information, see the steps in **Appendix A** at the end of this book.

1. Tap the **Settings** app, and then tap **General**.

2. Tap **Accessibility**, scroll down and tap **Home button** (but **DO NOT** press the actual **Home** button on your device), and then tap **Rest Finger to Open**.

After you have enabled this setting, you can press your finger on the **Home** button from the **Lock** screen and bypass the **Passcode** screen, to arrive immediately at your **Home** screen.

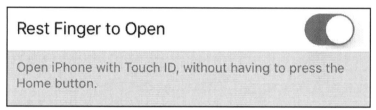

Figure 1.5: Rest finger to open setting

 Trick 3:

Get Immediate Access to the Camera App When Your Lock Screen is on

No longer do you have to worry about missing that perfect photo because you are stuck in **Lock**-screen mode. Past iOS upgrades have given you the ability to instantly access your camera with one quick swipe.

☐ **Swipe leftward** on the **Lock** screen or press the little camera icon to access your camera (see Figures 1.6 and 1.7).

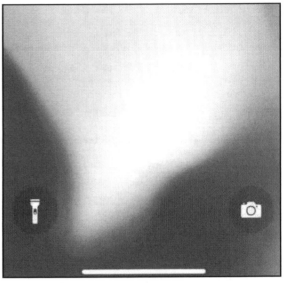

Figure 1.6: Accessing camera   Figure 1.7: Camera icon on iPhone X models

⭐ Trick 4:

Access Information from Your Lock Screen

Recent upgrades have brought other great **Lock** screen features, including the ability to instantly access information.

☐   **Swipe right** from the **Lock** screen to access widgets, certain apps, calendar, and more. (Swiping right also works from the **Home** screen to access widgets and more.)

☐   **Swipe down** on the **Lock** screen to see a cover sheet of notifications.

Note: We will cover more about notifications and widgets in a different part of this lesson.

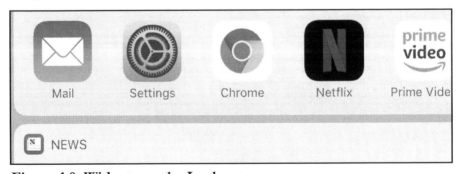

Figure 1.8: Widgets on the Lock screen

Trick 5:

Raise your iPhone/iPad to Wake It Before Unlocking (select models only)

You can raise your phone to wake it so that the **Lock** screen displays ASAP. This means that the display on your iPhone wakes up when you just raise your phone to look at it. Normally, you would have to press the **On/Off** button (or by other ways detailed earlier) to wake it each time. If you are on a phone call, for instance, the "awakened" phone call screen displays, and you can use the mute and other functions without pressing a button or unlocking.

Note: This trick involves changing a setting in the **Settings** app.

1. Tap the **Settings** app.

2. Tap **Display & Brightness**.

3. Scroll down until you locate the **Raise to Wake** selection.

4. Drag the white circle next to **Raise to Wake** to the right to enable it.

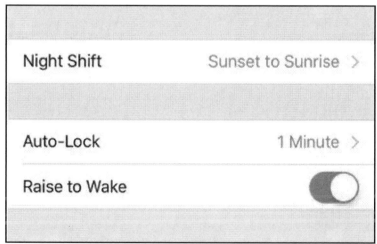

Figure 1.9: Raise to wake setting

Note: This trick may cause your device to light up (wake up) in a purse or pocket if it is jiggled and could result in significant battery drain. If this trick becomes more of a battery-draining issue than a time-saver, tap **Settings**, tap **Display and Brightness** and disable this selection by dragging the white circle switch to the left. To have the best of both worlds, you might look into purchasing an iPhone notebook case for extra screen protection.

Working with Lock Screen Widgets

You can get all the information you want from your **Lock** screen without having to unlock your device by using **widgets**. A **widget** is a limited app set up to display a specific amount of helpful information related to a larger application. In other words, it is not the full version of the app, just a partial extension, but it gives you information at a glance.

For instance, a **News** widget displays top headlines and a **Weather** widget shows temperatures, but neither has the full capabilities of the app they pull information from.

Figure 1.10: Widget

To display your existing widgets from the **Lock** screen:

1. Swipe to the right from your **Lock** screen to see your existing widgets.

2. Scroll down until you see **Edit** at the bottom, and then tap **Edit**.

3. Either use **Face ID**, rest your finger on the **Home** button in select models (if you programmed your fingerprint), or type in your **passcode** in order to arrive at the **Add Widget** screen.

Note: **Widgets** can also be accessed from the **Home** screen when you swipe right.

 Trick 6:

Add, Move, and Delete Lock Screen Widgets

The **Add Widgets** screen allows you to customize your widgets by adding, moving, and removing them. This screen is divided into two parts: **existing widgets** (denoted by a red minus sign) and **widgets you can add** (under the **More Widgets** section of the screen, denoted by a green plus sign).

Delete Existing Widgets

To delete existing **widgets**, perform these steps:

1. From the **Add Widgets** screen, tap the red minus sign next to an existing **widget**. The **widget** name slides left.

2. Tap the **Remove** button and the **widget** moves from the top group of existing **widgets** to the bottom area, under **More Widgets**.

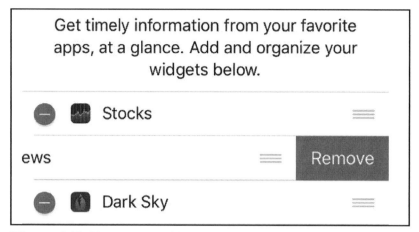

Figure 1.11: Remove a widget

Add More Widgets

To add a **widget** to the top group of existing widgets (widgets that display when you swipe to the right from the **Lock** screen or from the **Home** screen):

☐   Tap the green plus sign next to your desired widget under the **More Widgets** section of the page. The widget then displays in the top group of existing widgets.

Move Your Widgets

You can also move the widgets in the order you want to see them. For instance, if **News** is more important to you than **Weather,** and both are existing widgets, you can change the order of their appearance so that the **News** widget displays first.

To re-order your widgets:

1. Press down on the **move** symbol to the right of the widget name (see the circled icon in Figure 1.12), until it shows it is selected (by standing out from the background with a box around it).

2. Drag the widget to a desired location.

Figure 1.12: Move a widget

Trick 7:

Use 3D Touch to Access Quick Menus (select iPhone models only)

3D Touch is found on newer iPhone models (not iPhone 6 or earlier). **3D Touch** displays a menu of options (called **quick actions**) when you **long-press** (press down) on an app icon or a notification. Many apps display a **quick actions** menu following this **long-press**. Once the **quick-actions** menu displays, you can select one of the suggested actions on the fly. This prevents having to go through the usual app launching process, followed by drilling down through multiple menus.

Figure 1.13: 3D touch example

To perform this **3D Touch** trick:

1. From the **Lock** screen (or **Home** screen), swipe to the right to display your widgets.

2. Select a widget such as **Weather**, and **long-press** on the widget. The screen displays **quick actions** selections (see Figure 1.13).

3. Tap your preferred choice.

Note: You can **long-press** some app icons also.

Learn about Notifications

Group notifications are a great new feature of iOS 12. Any texts you receive on your **Lock** screen will display as an **iMessage** "group" alongside other types of notifications. You can expand the **iMessage** group with a tap and read all the grouped messages from your **Lock** screen. Also, you can easily open, view, or clear all notifications at once from your **Lock** screen, as shown in the next trick.

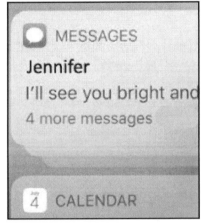

Figure 1.14 Group notices

 ## Trick 8:

Clear and Manage Notifications

To clear all notifications at once:

1. **Swipe down** on the **Lock** screen to access **Notification Center**, and then tap the "**X**", and a **Clear All Notifications** button displays.

2. Next, tap **Clear All Notifications**, and all notifications are cleared.

Figure 1.15: Clear all notifications

You can also swipe left and right to **View, Clear, Manage,** or **Open** each individual notification. To do so:

1. **Swipe down** from the top frame of the iPhone at the **Lock** screen to see notifications.

2. **Swipe right**, and then tap **Open** to open the app displaying the notification.

or

Swipe left, and then tap **View** or **Clear** to view the full notification or to clear each individual notification one at a time.

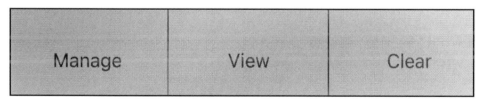

Figure 1.16: View or clear an individual notification

Tip: You can also use the **long-press** in the **Lock** screen to display **quick actions** menus for functions such as checking and returning your messages or emails – all when your phone is locked!

Note: You will see this "**X**" whether you have one or more messages or notifications.

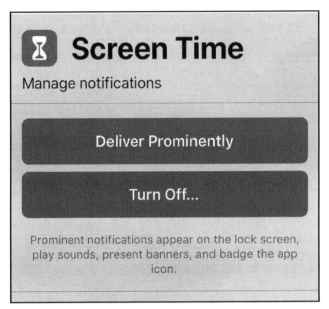

Figure 1.17 Manage notifications

To manage all notifications at once swipe left, and then tap **Manage** to set preferences for the way the app notifies you.

    In the **Manage** screen, you can also turn off alerts for a specific app or ask for notifications to be delivered quietly. In the future, they will appear in the **Notification Center**, but not on your **Lock** screen, and they won't play a sound or display a banner. You can also turn notifications back on by selecting **Deliver Prominently** in the **Manage Notifications** menu.

    You can also select **Deliver Quietly** to make alerts skip the lock screen and go to the **Notification Center**.

    We will cover more **3D Touch** tricks in the context of the updated **Control Center** in the next chapter.

Control Center Updates & Tricks

2

Control Center Update

Control Center was redesigned in the last update, and there were many changes. To review them, access **Control Center** by **swiping down from the top right corner** of iPhone X models (and iP ads using iOS 12), or by **swiping up from the bottom frame** (on earlier devices and earlier iOS versions).

Note: When you are done with **Control Center,** exit by swiping back up or down.

Figure 2.1: Control Center

Note that in **Control Center**, icons (called **controls** or **tiles**), are grouped in separate **panels**. Many of these **panels** can be expanded to show additional controls when you perform a **long-press** on them. You can tap a control to turn the control on and tap again to turn the control off. You can also customize **Control Center** by adding or removing certain controls.

Parts of Control Center

In Figure 2.1, **Control Center** controls are identified by numbers:

❑   **Airplane** mode – (1) Tapping the airplane control turns on **Airplane** mode which turns off **wireless** and **cellular** signals in addition to **Bluetooth**. **Airplane** mode was originally created as a quick way to turn off reception in response to airline restrictions.

Tip: In **Control Center**, turn off **Airplane** mode, and then turn **Wi-Fi** and **Bluetooth** back on, even when the **cellular** signal is still off. This is a way to conserve battery power on your device, but you won't receive calls.

Tip: You can charge your phone much faster when you turn on **Airplane** mode when charging. If you are in a hurry and have to charge your phone at the last minute, don't forget **Airplane** mode! However, you won't be able to receive calls/emails in **Airplane** mode, so turn it back on when done.

❑   **Cellular mode** – (2) This control, when selected, shows that you are connected to a cellular network.

❑   **Wi-Fi mode** – (3) This control, when selected, shows that you are connected to Wi-Fi.

❑   **Bluetooth** mode – (4) **Bluetooth** is a wireless technology for data exchange over short distances between devices. An example of **Bluetooth** technology is the pairing in the car between your phone and the car's speakers for hands-free calling when driving.

Customizing Control Center

The ability to customize parts of **Control Center** was a brand-new feature of the last iOS upgrade. **Control Center** could also be called the "shortcut center," and as such, some shortcuts valued by some users may not be important to others. We can add/remove specific controls, based on our own user preferences, as illustrated in later sections.

Expanding Control Center Panels

When you tap certain **Control Center** panels, they **expand** to display additional controls. This is explored in the next trick which introduces **Night Shift** mode.

Figure 2.2: Expanded brightness panel

 Trick 9:

Enable Night Shift Mode to Protect Your Eyesight at Night

Night Shift automatically changes the colors of your screen to warmer hues after dark. This feature cuts out your nightly exposure to the blue light that emanates from devices. Prolonged exposure to blue light can suppress the production of melatonin and disrupt the sleeping process.

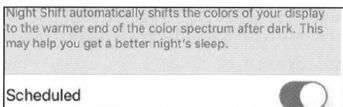

Figure 2.3: Night Shift mode

To set up **Night Shift** mode:

1. Tap the **Settings** app, and then tap **Display & Brightness**.

2. Tap **Night Shift**. Move the white circle next to **Scheduled** to the right.

Note: You can set specific time periods in the **From/To** area and enable the **Manually Enable Until Tomorrow** setting when you want to turn it on manually. You can also adjust the color temperature in this screen.

Note: After you have set up **Night Shift** mode in **Settings**, you can enable or disable **Night Shift** mode from **Control Center** by **long-pressing** the **Brightness** control - (11), and then tapping the **Night Shift** control.

Flashlight

The **Flashlight** (8) is a very popular feature, and being able to access it quickly in **Control Center** has only increased its ease of use. However, its conspicuous bright beam can be embarrassing in such settings as restaurants. No longer! You can adjust the **Flashlight** settings, so you can change to a low or medium light setting. Below is a trick for this!

Figure 2.4: Flashlight brightness modes

 # Trick 10:

Quickly choose between Flashlight Brightness Settings on Your iPhone

To perform this trick, follow these instructions:

1. Access **Control Center**. (See the beginning of this chapter for how to access **Control Center**.)

2. Next, **long-press** on the **Flashlight** control. A graphic displays several segments that start from low light (bottom) to high brightness (top).

3. Tap any of these segments, as shown in Figure 2.4, in order to set the **Flashlight's** brightness level.

Clock

There have been new changes to the **Clock** app in recent updates. A **Bedtime** mode displayed at the bottom menu bar of the **Clock** app lets you control your sleep time, and the sounds you want to wake up to.

Tip: You can reach the **Clock** app by tapping the shortcut control in **Control Center**, or you can navigate and tap the **Clock** app in your **Home** screen.

 # Trick 11:

Turn on the Bedtime Mode in the Clock App

Bedtime mode in the **Clock** app lets you customize your waking and sleeping times.

To set up **Bedtime** mode in the **Clock** app:

1. Open the **Clock** app, and then tap **Bedtime** in the bottom menu bar.

2. Tap **Get Started**, and then select your desired wake-up time.

3. Tap **Next**, and then select the days when your alarm should go off.

4. Tap **Next**, and then choose how many hours of sleep you want.

5. Tap **Next**, and then set your **Bedtime** reminder time.

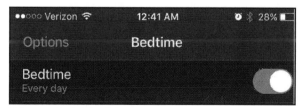

Figure 2.5: Bedtime app

6. Tap **Next,** and then select your wake-up sound.

7. Tap **Next**, and then tap **Save** in the upper right corner of the screen. To change **Bedtime** settings, tap the **Options** button in the upper left corner of the screen, and then tap **Done**.

To change the hours, move **the moon icon** (for bedtime changes) and/or **the bell icon** (for wake-up changes). To enable or disable this feature, move the white circle to the right or left.

iOS 12 has linked **Bedtime** mode to the **Do Not Disturb** feature (see **Trick 83**). If you navigate from the **Home** screen to **Settings**, and **Do Not Disturb**, then move the white circle to the right, calls and notifications will be silenced and your notifications will bypass the **Lock** screen.

This means if you glance at your phone during the night, you won't see a list of pending distractions. Only when you wake up in the morning will you see a list of everything that happened overnight.

Additional Control Center Controls

❏ **Orientation lock** – (5) First, orient your device the way you prefer, then bring up **Control Center**, and tap the **Orientation** lock control to lock the orientation to either portrait or landscape.

❏ **Do Not Disturb mode** – (6) With **Do Not Disturb** mode on, you can silence calls, alerts, and notifications from coming in while your device is locked. If don't want to be disturbed, such as when sleeping, you can create a schedule. To do so, tap **Settings**, tap **Do Not Disturb**, and enable **Scheduled**. Set the hours to not be disturbed (and program who can disturb you in emergencies).

❏ **Brightness slider bar** – (11) Brightens/darkens your screen.

❏ **Music/Audio controls** – (10) Displays the **Rewind, Play/Pause**, and **Fast Forward** icons. **Note: Pause** displays when **Play** is tapped a second time, and pauses the audio.

❏ **Volume slider bar** – (12) Adjusts volume from low to high.

❏ **Screen Mirroring** – (7) Formerly called **AirPlay**, this feature allows you to connect to an **Apple TV** device by tapping the **Apple TV** selection (instead of the **iPad** or **iPhone** selections) so that what displays on your iPhone/iPad screen is "cast" outward and displays on your TV.

❏ **Timer** – (9) Allows you to program timed segments and alarms.

❐   **Calculator** – (13) Brings up the **Calculator** app.

❐   **Camera** – (14) Brings up the **Camera** app.

More Control Center Controls

Here are some extra controls that you can add to your **Control Center** page. **Trick 12** (below) shows how you can add controls to **Control Center**.

❐   **QR code reader** – A QR (Quick Response) code is a type of bar-code with information that can be read by a scanning system. QR codes are everywhere, from signs to magazine ads to online web-sites. Just pointing your camera at a QR code translates the code, but in iOS 12 you can add this control to **Control Center** to quickly access this feature. To use the QR reader, see **Trick 27**.

❐   **Low Power mode** – When you turn on low power mode, you can extend the battery life of your device. Adding this control to **Control Center** makes it easy to turn on and off.

❐   **Text Size** – You can adjust text sizes that display on your device.

❐   **Magnifier** – You can add **Magnifier** to **Control Center** (see **Trick 12**). Tap the control to turn it on. Tap again to turn it off.

❐   **Screen Recording** – This excellent feature allows you to make a video recording of actions happening on your device's screen.

❐   **Alarm** – Access alarms via **Control Center** instead of in **Clock**.

❐   **Accessibility Shortcuts** – You can access accessibility shortcuts such as **VoiceOver, Zoom**, and more in **Control Center**.

❐   **Apple TV Remote** – Turn your device into a TV remote.

❐   **Do Not Disturb While Driving** – Lets you block texts, calls, etc. when driving.

❐   **Guided Access** – Limits users to using one specific app, and will not let you switch to another app or to the **Home** screen.

❐   **Hearing Aids**– Pairs with your hearing aids to program changes.

❐   **Voice Memos** – Allows your device to record voice dictations. See **Trick 97**.

❐   **Wallet** – Lets you store coupons, boarding passes, tickets, store cards, credit cards, and debit cards and use **Apple Pay Cash** to pay. In iOS 12, student ID cards can be stored in the **Wallet** app, which gives access to dorms, dinners, libraries, laundry, and more.

Trick 12:

Add the Text Size and Magnifier Controls to Control Center

To add the **Text Size** and **Magnifier** controls to **Control Center**:

1. From the **Home** screen, tap the **Settings** app, tap **Control Center**, and then tap **Customize Controls**.

2. Add the **Text Size** and **Magnifier** controls to **Control Center** by tapping the green plus sign under the **More Controls** section of the page in the lower area. The controls then display in the top group of controls listed under **Include**.

Note: To remove a control from **Control Center**, tap the red minus sign next to the control you want to remove that is listed under the top **Include** section on the page. The control then displays in the bottom group of unused controls under **More Controls**.

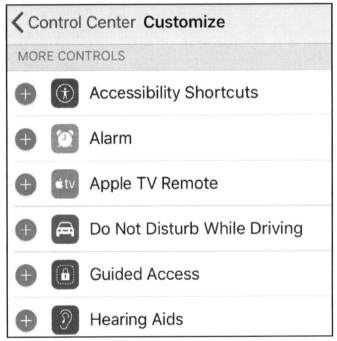

Figure 2.6: Add a Control

The next chapter spotlights tricks for Apple's **Home**, **TV**, **Books**, and **Files** apps.

Apple Updated Apps & Tricks To Use Them

3

The Apple apps that debuted in recent updates have been further improved in iOS 12, making it easier to control your home appliances, your home entertainment, and your file storage needs.

The Apple Home App

Apple provided a new app in a past update called **Home** that let you set up your smart home appliances (from **HomeKit** approved vendors) under one umbrella. With Apple **Home**, you can:

❑   **Add HomeKit-approved smart appliances** such as smart thermostats, light bulbs, door locks, and more (called accessories) to your **Home** app.

❑   **Control your accessories** through **Siri** who can notify you about your accessories on your **Lock** screen.

The **Home** app also integrates with Apple **TV**, allowing remote access so you can turn on lights, even when you are not at home. This app also supports geofencing, which is the ability to

 create a geographic boundary, so that specific smart gadgets can be triggered to turn on or off as you pull up to your house.

Figure 3.1: Apple Home app

Connecting Your Smart Appliances

You can connect your smart appliances to the **Home** app, and also add the **Home** app control to **Control Center** to easily manage your **Accessories**.

 Trick 13:

Add Your Smart Accessory to the Home App

Note: To start using the Apple **Home** app, you need to have smart accessories that you can add to a list there. Go to www.apple.com to find out if your appliance is listed in the **HomeKit**-approved accessories.

To add your smart devices to the Apple **Home** app list:

1. Turn on any nearby lights, locks, thermostats, or other devices approved by Apple.

2. Tap the **Home** app and then tap **Add Accessory**. If it is an approved accessory, you can look for the code on the accessory or hold the phone near the accessory label in some cases for it to be recognized.

3. Tap a listed accessory, and then follow the on-screen prompts.

4. Next, you will be asked to name each accessory. You can also name the room it is in.

5. Tap **Next** to finish, and then tap **Done**.

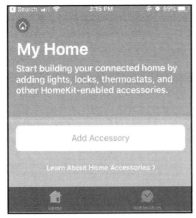

Figure 3.2: Add an accessory

Tricks to Use Them

Understanding Scenes

Scenes let you control multiple accessories at the same time. For example, you might create a scene called **Arrive Home** that turns on your lights, adjusts the thermostat, and unlocks the front door – accomplished only when you reach your driveway.

 # Trick 14:

Create a Scene in Apple Home

To create a scene:

1. Open the **Home** app, and tap **Rooms** in the bottom menu bar.

2. Tap **+**.

3. Tap **Add Scene**, add a **Scene Name**, add all or some of the listed accessories to this scene, and then tap **Done**.

Figure 3.3: Apple Home control added to Control Center

Tip: You can **long-press** an accessory to adjust its settings if you have a newer iPhone model that supports **3D Touch**. To preview the changes to your new scene, tap **Test This Scene**.

To be able to access your scenes from **Control Center,** tap **Turn on Show in Favorites** in that menu. Tap **Done** to finish the process of adding the **Home** control to the **Control Center**.

Apple's TV App

Apple's **TV** app lets you watch TV shows and movies from many different entertainment vendors in one central place. The opening menus in the **TV** app don't just display Apple apps like iTunes, but also include streaming channels such as HBO Now, and others. The **TV** app's **Watch Now** screen displays a list of available shows. However, you may not find Amazon offered in any Apple TV channel. You also may not find the Netflix channel in the **Store** option in the bottom menu bar, but you can add shows found on Netflix by searching for the desired title.

Trick 15:

Open the TV App on Any of Your Devices to Find Information about Your Shows

To open the **TV** app on any of your devices to find information about the titles you added to your list:

1. Tap the Apple **TV** app.

2. Tap **Watch Now,** and you can view all the current available movies and TV shows in your list, along with the progress of your viewing sessions for each title.

Figure 3.4: Apple's TV app

The Apple TV Screens

Apple **TV** app menus include the following:

❑ **Watch Now**: This screen is where viewers can see their list of available shows and movies from iTunes and many other entertainment vendors. The **Up Next** section in this menu displays your current TV shows and movies.

❑ **Library**: You can view your rented or purchased iTunes titles here.

❑ **Store**: You can shop at the **Store** to find searchable titles from different entertainment vendors.

❑**Search**:   You   can   search   the   app   for   titles   and   more.

Figure 3.5: Watch Now screen

The iOS 12 update has introduced a new feature that allows you to add the Apple **TV** control to **Control Center**. For more information on how to add a control to **Control Center**, see **Chapter 2**. In iOS 12, the Apple **TV** app will also send notifications to you when a new episode in the **Up Next** queue is available to watch.

The Apple Files App

The **Files** app lets all of your files display in one place instead of having to locate them in different apps. These files can be files that are on your device, or files located in **iCloud Drive.** Note that **iCloud Drive** allows all of your different devices to access a file (and other people you choose to share with). The **Files** app also supports such third-party cloud services as **Dropbox** and **Google Drive**, to truly consolidate all your apps that contain files. In addition, the **Files** app allows you to organize files, and also to tag them by name and color.

 # Trick 16:

Save an Email Attachment to the iCloud Drive folder in the Files App

To save an email attachment to the **iCloud Drive** folder in the **Files** app:

1. Locate an email that contains an attachment, and then press and hold the attachment until the **Share** menu displays.

2. Tap **Save to Files**, and then tap **iCloud Drive**. If any folders appear, you may choose to tap on one of the existing **iCloud Drive** folders.

3. Tap **Add** in the upper right corner of the screen.

To see the file:

1. Go back to the **Home** screen, and tap the **Files** app.

2. Next, tap the **iCloud Drive** folder. Your file should appear in this folder.

Figure 3.6: Files app

Figure 3.7: Books app

The Apple Books App

In iOS 12, Apple's **Books** app replaces the former **iBooks** app with a complete redesign. There is a new **Reading Now** tab that shows the books that you are currently reading (or listening to). There is a **Want to Read** section that lets you curate your own "wishlist" of books to read in the future. There are suggestions such as **Complete the Series** or **You Might Like** which offer suggested titles based on those you have recently finished.

There is an **Audiobooks** tab, which allows you to listen to books, whether at home or when using **CarPlay** while driving.

The **Book Store** tab lets you browse all available books and multiple genres, and you can narrow the search using Apple-created categories such as **Top Charts**, **Staff Picks**, and more. In addition, Apple offers recommendations based on your past purchases in the **For You** section.

The **Library** tab lets you access the books you have purchased and/or downloaded, with information about how far you read into each book. If you completed the book, you can check out the **Finished** section, which comes complete with a timeline that graphically depicts your reading history.

If you are a committed reader, be sure and check out the revamped Apple **Books** app, and peruse all the bells and whistles that have been added in the iOS 12 update!

The next chapter covers recent updates and changes to Apple's **Photos** and **Camera** apps.

Updates to Apple's Photos and Camera Apps

4

Recent upgrades have brought in major additions to Apple's **Photos** and **Camera** apps.

Changes to the Photos App

In iOS 12, the **Photo** app has been redesigned. In addition, photos on the iPhone/iPad are now scanned with more sophisticated **facial recognition** technology. People are automatically sorted into a **People** album. You can identify people so they can be grouped together and searched by name in the future.

The New Photos App Menu Bar

In iOS 12, the menu bar is divided into these categories:

- ☐ **Photos** – This mode allows you to look at your photos grouped by day or several days or the years in which they were taken.

- ☐ **For You** – This mode features selected "memory" slideshows along with sharing suggestions for your contacts who may be in those photos and memories.

- ☐ **Albums** – This mode allows you to see your photos grouped into albums such as the **All Photos**, **Recently Deleted**, and more, plus the albums you created.

> ❑   **Search** – This new mode features a powerful search tool that will let you search for photos by such criteria as location, event, people, and even animals! You can also type in multiple search terms.

The next trick tells you how to identify people in your photos by name, so you can take advantage of Apple's advanced facial recognition technology.

Figure 4.1: iOS 12 Menu Bar

 # Trick 17:

Identify People in Photos for Searches

Here's how to identify people in photos for future searches!

Note: If your photo is a **Live Photo** (see more about **Live Photos** later in this chapter), you must make a still-photo copy first. To do so, tap the **Share** icon, tap **Duplicate**, tap **Duplicate as Still Photo**, and then scroll through **All Photos** to find your new still photo before starting this trick.

1. Tap the **Photos** app, and tap **Albums** in the menu bar at the bottom.

2. Tap the **All Photos** (or **Camera Roll**) album and select a photo of the person you want to identify for future searches by name.

3. Swipe upwards from mid-screen and you will see the individual faces from that photo broken out into little squares.

4. Tap the face square of the person that you want to identify, and the **Add Name** screen displays. Next, tap **Add Name** at the top.

5. Type in the name of the person, and then tap **Next**. The person will be confirmed on the next screen, and you can exit out of the menu by pressing **Done**.

> ❑   **People album** – You can find this named person by navigating to the main **Albums** screen, and tapping the **People** album.

> ❑   **Search mode** – Tap the **Search** mode on the **Photo** app menu bar, and type in the person's name to access their photos.

Figure 4.2: Identify and name people in photos

Learn about Memories

Memories are photographic slideshows automatically created for you by Apple. They can include clips from video and music.

 # Trick 18:

Play and Edit Memories

To play and edit the memories prepared for you:

1. Tap the **Photos** app from the **Home** screen.

2. Tap **For You** on the menu bar at the bottom of the screen to access your curated **memories**. You will see numerous slideshows created for you.

3. Tap on one of the **Memories** that Apple has already created for you. The **Main Menu** of this particular **Memory** displays.

4. Press the **Play** icon on the slideshow. The screen displays a downloading icon, and then once it has downloaded, the **Memory** will play.

5. To make changes, tap the screen, and then press the **Pause** button at the bottom to pause the show. You are now in the **Pause** mode screen.

6. Next, tap **Edit** at the top. You will see the following:

   ☐   **Title** – Tap this selection to change your title on the first slide.

   ☐   **Music** – Tap this selection to change the music.

   ☐   **Duration** – Tap this selection to change the length of the film.

   ☐   **Photos & Videos** – Tap this selection to add or remove photos.

7. Tap **Done** when you have made adjustments. You will arrive back in the **Pause** mode screen where you can either press the **Play** button, the **Back** (<) blue link at the top, or the **Home** button to exit (on iPads/iPhone 8/8 Plus iPhones) or **swipe up from the base** (on iPhone X models).

Figure 4.3: Memory edit screen

In the **Pause** mode screen, you can also make these selections:

❑   Select the **Short** or **Medium** choices to set the length of time for the slideshow.

❑   Select the **font** choices (**Happy, Uplifting** etc.) for the fonts.

Figure 4.4: Change fonts and duration

 Trick 19:

Save and Delete Photos from Your Slideshow

To save your slideshow:

1. Tap the **Photos** app from the **Home** screen.

2. Tap **For You** on the menu bar at the bottom of the screen to access your **memories**. You will see numerous slideshows created for you.

3. Tap on one of the **Memories** that Apple has created for you. The **Main Menu** of this particular **Memory** displays.

4. Press **Play** on the slideshow. The screen will display a downloading icon, and then when the progress reaches 100%, the **Memory** plays.

5. Tap the screen once to return to the **Pause** menu.

6. Press the **Pause** button to pause the show. You are now in the **Pause** mode screen.

7. Tap the **Share** button in the lower left corner of the screen, and then tap **Save Video**. It will appear in the **Videos** album in the **Photos** app.

Delete Photos from Your Memory

To delete photos from your slideshows, perform these steps:

1. Tap the **Photos** app from the **Home** screen.

2. Tap **For You** on the menu bar at the bottom of the screen to access your **memories**. You will see numerous slideshows created for you.

3. Tap one of the **Memories**. The **Main Menu** of this particular **Memory** displays.

4. Press the **Play** icon on the slideshow. The screen displays a downloading icon, and then once it has downloaded, the **Memory** will play.

Figure 4.5: Delete photos in a Memory slideshow

5. To make changes, tap the screen, and then press the **Pause** button at the bottom to pause the show. You are now in the **Pause** mode screen.

6. Next, tap **Edit** at the top, and then tap **Photos & Videos**.

7. Scroll through the pictures, and then tap the garbage can icon to delete the photos that you do not want in the particular **Memory**.

Delete a Memory From Your Memory Collection

To delete a **Memory**, perform the following steps.

1. Tap the **Photos** app from the **Home** screen.

2. Tap **For You** on the menu bar at the bottom of the screen to access your **memories**.

3. Tap on one of the **Memories** that Apple has already created for you. This is the **Main Menu** of this particular **Memory**.

4. Scroll until you reach the bottom of the screen.

5. Tap **Delete Memory**, and then tap **Delete Memory** again.

Trick 20:

Make Your Memory a Favorite

You can add a **Memory** to a **Favorite Memories** album that is located in **Album** mode. This makes it easily accessible, and saves time. Otherwise, you must page through all the **Memories** prepared for you. Here's how!

1. Tap the **Photos** app from the **Home** screen.

2. Tap **For You** on the menu bar at the bottom of the screen to access your **memories**. You will see numerous slideshows created for you.

3. Tap one of the **Memories** that Apple has created for you. The **Main Menu** of that particular **Memory** displays.

4. Scroll to the bottom of the screen, and tap **Add to Favorite Memories.**

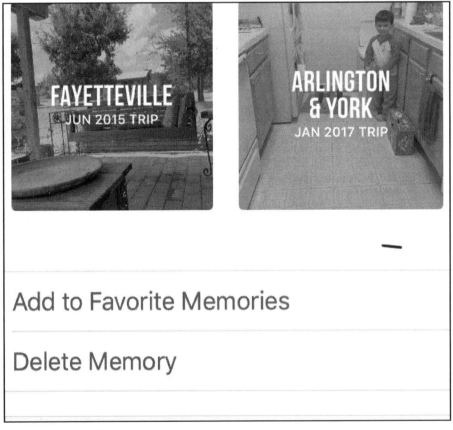

Figure 4.6: Add to Favorite Memories

 Trick 21:

Create Your Own Memory

You can create your own **Memory** instead of waiting for Apple to create automatic **Memories**. To do so:

1. Tap the **Photos** app and then tap **Albums** (on the bottom right of the menu bar). Look for the + in the upper left corner. It should say **Albums** at the top of the screen.

2. Tap the **+** sign and type in a new **Album** name.

3. Tap the pictures you want to add to this album (and subsequent **Memory**), and then tap **Done**.

4. Open the new album and tap the **day or date range** listed at the top of the screen. Next, tap the **Play** button to create the **Memory**. It will begin.

5. Next, tap the video to pause it, tap the **< (Back)** button, and then scroll down to the bottom of the page and tap **Add to Memory**.

Congratulations! You have created a **Memory** slideshow! You can edit it further in the **Memories** section, as described earlier in this chapter.

Changes to Apple's Camera App

Recent upgrades brought enhancements to the **Camera** app, including the ability to create special effects for your **Live Photos**. You can also play with the new **Live Photo** feature in the **Facetime** app, which lets either party in the conversation take a live photo during the video conversation. You can turn off **Facetime's Live Photo** in the **Settings > Facetime** menu.

Live Photo Editing

Note: **Live Photo** only works on the iPhone 6S and newer models, but a live photo created by another person can be viewed by older iPhones.

Live Photo is a **Camera** app feature that captures a few seconds of video and audio before and after taking a still photo on your iPhone. Use **Live Photo** when you want to capture simple motion in your photo. Turn this feature on only when you want to create a non-still photo. If the bulls-eye is yellow in your **Camera** app, **Live Photo** is on. Tap it once to turn it off.

Figure 4.7: Live Photo "bulls-eye" icon

 Trick 22:

Edit Live Photos

The last update added a feature to add effects like **Bounce, Loop,** and **Long Exposure** to your **Live Photos**. In addition, you can turn **Live Photos** into **still** photos. To edit **Live Photos**:

1. Take a photo using your **Camera** app in **Photo** mode, making sure the **Live Photo** bulls-eye icon is yellow.

2. From the **Home** screen, launch the **Photos** app, select **Albums** mode, select **All Photos**, and then select the live photo you took. You can edit with the brightness, cropping, enhancing, filtering tools and more.

3. Tap **Done** when you are finished and swipe down from the top to return to the **Camera** app.

Note: Since a **Live Photo** is actually many photos, you can press down on the one that you want to designate as the identifying photo, and select **Make Keynote Photo**.

Note: To turn a **Live Photo** into a still photo, make sure you are in **Edit** mode (as described above), and then select the still photo you prefer out of the series displayed at the bottom. Tap **Make Keynote Photo**, and then tap the orange-colored **Live** icon at the bottom right. The icon will display as **Off**. Tap **Done**, and the photo becomes a still photo.

 Trick 23:

Add Special Effects for Live Photos

To create loops and bounce effects for your **Live Photos**:

1. Open the **Photos** app and tap **Albums** on the bottom menu bar.

2. Select a **Live Photo**, and then swipe upwards from mid-screen to select an effect from the **Effects** list: **Live, Loop, Bounce, Long Exposure**.

Figure 4.8: Portrait mode   **Figure 4.9: Lighting effect**

Work with Portrait Mode (select models)

Portrait mode, available on iPhone 7 and select other models, lets you take a stunning portrait by blurring the background, which strongly delineates the person being photographed. iOS 12 has updated **Portrait** mode in ways that improve results even further. By generating a mask once a person is identified, **Portrait** mode now seamlessly separates the subject from the background. Other enhancements include **OIS** (optical image stabilization), new **flash** capability, and **Portrait Lighting** (iPhone 8 Plus/X models). Also included is the high dynamic resolution (**HDR**) feature which now works with **Portrait** mode. **HDR** automatically combines three exposures of a photo (dark, light, normal) to create a vivid and rich final snapshot.

 Trick 24:

Use Portrait Mode

To work with **Portrait** mode, follow these instructions

1. Open the **Camera** app.

2. Scroll through the modes (**Photo, Video**, etc), and then select **Portrait**.

Tip: To take the best photos in **Portrait** mode:

☐   Make sure the subject is in a brightly-lit environment.

☐   Make sure the person is not too close to you because the further away the person is from the background, the stronger the blur effect.

☐   Make sure the background contains bright colors to ensure better contrast.

Trick 25:

Mark Up a Photo

iOS 12 introduces more colors to this very important feature, allowing you to annotate and draw on your photos.

Note: Marking up a **Live Photo** turns it into a still photo. If you want to avoid this, make a still-photo copy of the **Live Photo** to mark up (see **Trick 22**).

1. Go to the **Photos** app, tap **Albums**, and then tap a photo.

2. Tap **Share**, tap **Duplicate**, and then tap **Duplicate as still photo**.

3. Navigate to the latest photos to locate the duplicated photo and then follow the instructions below to mark up your still photo.

To mark up a photo:

1. Go to the **Photos** app, tap **Albums**, and then tap a photo.

2. Tap **Edit**, and then tap the **More** button (three vertical dots at the bottom right).

3. Tap **Markup**, tap the double-ringed circle to get colors, tap a marker, and then use your finger to draw around the photo. You can use text boxes to annotate drawings and more.

4. Tap **Done** when you are done.

Figure 4.10: Mark up a photo

Trick 26:

Work with Screenshots

Screenshots can be very valuable to capture error messages, text conversation selections, and more. iOS 12 has added a feature to prevent accidental screenshots when the display is turned of on certain models.

1. Press the **On/Off** button at the exact same time as the **Home** button (iPads/iPhone 8/8 Plus and earlier models) or press the **Volume Up** button at the same time as the **On/Off** button (iPhone X, XS/Max, XR models). A thumbnail photo displays in the lower-right corner.

2. Tap the photo to look at it, draw on it, or delete it. You can use drawing tools to annotate this photo. To delete or save the screenshot to the **Photos** app, tap **Done**, and tap either **Delete** or **Save to Photos**.

Note: If you want to keep the screenshot without looking at it, quickly swipe to the left or leave it alone for some seconds and the screenshot will be transferred directly to the **Photos** app.

3. To locate your photo in the **Photos** app, return to the **Home** screen, tap the **Photos** app icon, tap **Albums** in the bottom menu bar, and then tap the **All Photos** or **Camera Roll** album (it will also display in the **Screenshots** album).

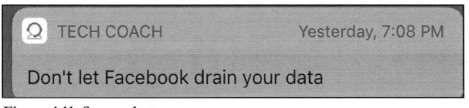

Figure 4.11: Screenshot

 # Trick 27:

Experience the QR Code Camera Feature

A QR (Quick Response) code is a type of barcode with information that can be read by a scanning system. QR codes are everywhere, from real estate signs to magazines to online websites. The last update gave the **Camera** app the ability to interpret QR codes by simply aiming the camera at them. Here's how!

Figure 4.12: QR Code for iWorkshopacademy.com

1. Tap the **Camera** app, and make sure you are in **Photo** mode (in the bottom mode bar).

2. Point the camera at the above QR code (or any other QR code you may have in your possession such as a flyer or a real estate brochure), and then wait for the message to appear at the top of the screen.

3. Tap the message and you will be taken to the website or application that is referenced by the QR code.

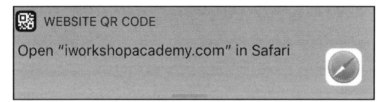

Figure 4.13: QR Identification Message Example

Note: In iOS 12, you can add the QR feature to **Control Center** instead of just accessing it by launching the **Camera** app. See **Chapter 2** to review the instructions on how to add a new control to **Control Center**.

Note: You can also access the QR code-reading feature by **long-pressing** the **Camera** app icon, which gives you several choices including **Scan QR Code**.

Texting App Tricks

5

Of all the changes brought by the last operating system upgrades, the biggest overhaul happened to **iMessage**, Apple's **texting** app. These changes enable you to access your apps to insert images, videos, and preset animations such as balloons and confetti into your text messages using the **App Drawer** toolbar at the bottom of the screen.

> **Tip**: The **App Drawer** toolbar does not have to display on your screen at all times when texting. To make it disappear, just tap the **App Store** icon immediately to the left of the text message box. The **App Drawer** disappears until you tap the **App Store** icon again.

Figure 5.1: App Drawer

Animation effects

You can add **animations** to your text messages very easily. When you type a message, instead of tapping on the blue **Send** arrow, perform a **long-press** on it to see all the options.

A list of choices displays with the following animations you can add to your text bubbles:

- ☐ **Slam**: Receiver sees your message bubble "slam" on the screen.

- ☐ **Loud**: Receiver sees your message grow bigger.

- ☐ **Gentle**: Receiver sees your message grow smaller.

- ☐ **Invisible Ink**: Receiver must swipe the bubble to see the message.

 # Trick 28:

Use Screen Mode to Send Exciting Animations

To send text messages with bubbles, confetti and more:

1. Type your message and then perform a **long-press** on the blue **Send** arrow. Tap the word **Screen** at the top and you will see one of the animations.

2. Swipe to the left to see other animations that can accompany your message, such as spotlight, echo, confetti, heart, lasers, and others.

Note: These messages display completely for iPhone/iPad users, but only show text (e.g. the word "Balloons") for those with devices running on non-Apple operating systems.

3. Either tap the **Send** arrow to send your text with the animations or tap **X** to cancel to get out of the animations screen.

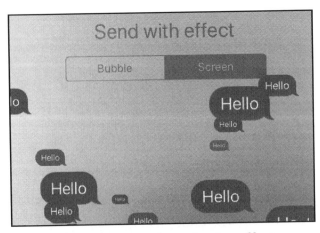

Figure 5.2: Screen mode and echo effect

Trick 29:

Create a Handwritten Message When Texting

The personal touch can add to the fun when texting, and to that end, you can create **handwritten** messages to send when texting. Here's how.

1. Tap the **iMessage** texting app.

2. Rotate your phone to landscape mode and tap the **curlicue** icon in the bottom right corner.

3. Write out your message with your finger, then tap the **Send** arrow. You can also use one of the stock messages that are already created and that display various styles of cursive writing (see Figure 5.3).

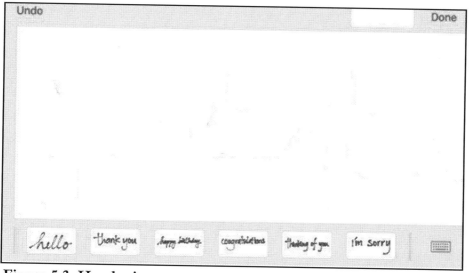

Figure 5.3: Handwritten messages

Fellow iOS users will see an animation that looks like you are writing it in real time. Non-iOS users will receive a handwritten image.

Tip: You can also send emails displaying handwriting by **long-pressing** on an email screen and then swiping left (past the **Select** and **Select All** selections) until you can tap the **Insert Drawing** selection. At this point you can use your finger to write or draw something within your email. In addition, you can add handwritten messages in the **Notes** app by tapping the pencil icon at the bottom and moving your finger. They are searchable in **Spotlight Search** (swipe down at the **Home** screen and type in keywords to search).

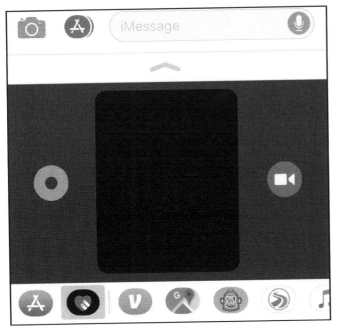

Figure 5.4: iMessage drawing tools

 Trick 30:

Using Digital Touch to Draw in Your Messages

Past upgrades relocated **Digital Touch** to the new **App Drawer**. **Digital Touch** allows you to **create drawings**, and to use **gestures**. **Gestures** are pre-fabricated sets of animations (kisses, fireballs) that you can call up by tapping in a specific way.

Here's how to use **Digital Touch**:

1. Tap the **App Store** icon to the left of the text message area to bring up the **App Drawer**.

2. Tap the **Digital Touch heart** icon to display the drawing tools.

   ☐ To make a drawing or a doodle, tap the orange circle on the left, tap a color, and make a little sketch in the black box. If you want to send it out, tap the blue **Send** arrow in the black box.

Note: If you need more screen space, tap the up arrow at the bottom right to expand to full-screen.

Figure 5.5: Video and digital gesture info icons

❏   To send animated **Digital Touch** messages by using **gestures** using the same black box, either tap or tap and hold on the black box as follows:

Note: A digital touch drawing will be sent out right away. If you play around with the following gestures, be aware that they will be sent to the recipient **immediately** after you perform the action to create them.

❏ **Tap:** Tap with one finger to send a tap animation.

❏ **Fireball: Long-press** to send a fireball animation.

❏ **Kiss:** Tap with two fingers to send a kiss.

❏ **Heartbeat:** Tap and hold with two fingers to send a heartbeat.

❏ **Heartbreak:** Tap and hold with two fingers, then drag down.

Note: A digital touch drawing will disappear from your text message in two minutes, unless you tap **Keep**, which displays under the drawing. The **Keep** option means that this drawing will not be removed from the text conversation. If you want to save your drawing, immediately **long-press** the drawing, select **Copy**, and then bring up an image app or another texting app such as **What's App** or Facebook's **Messenger** to paste it in. However, the copied gesture or drawing will not be animated in another program.

Tip: You can sketch on top of video and photos using drawing tools or gestures by tapping the camera icon and then drawing on top of the image/video.

Tip: You can take a photo by pressing the photo button on the left, and then draw on top of it. You can add the above-listed gestures to photos.

To exit the drawing tools, and remove the **App Drawer** from view, simply tap the **App Store** button.

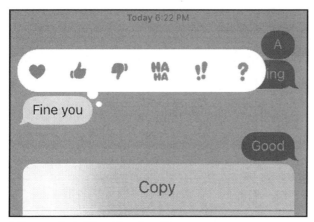

Figure 5.6: Tap Back a Response

 Trick 31:

Send Quick Responses with a Tap Back

You can add **quick responses** for when you don't have the time to type out a text response.

To perform a quick response:

1. Tap and hold on a message you've received. A pop-up will show options such as a heart, thumbs up/down, haha, !!, or ? (see Figure 5.7).

2. Tap one of the icons. The quick response will attach directly to the message.

Figure 5.7: Quick Response

Note: A new iOS 12 feature lets you tap back on **iMessage** notifications that display on your **Lock** screen. When you receive a text notification on the **Lock** screen, **long-press** to reply and then tap and hold on the message to select a tap back response.

Trick 32:

Tap to Replace Words with Emojis

Once you've typed out a message, you can easily search to see if any words can be replaced with emojis. Here's how!

1. Type your message, then tap the **emoji** button at the bottom.

2. The **iMessage** app highlights any word in red that can be replaced with an emoji.

3. Press down on the word and then tap the emoji you want to use. It will replace the word that you typed in.

Figure 5.8: Emojis

 # Trick 33:

Locate and Download Extra Apps to Add Your Own Stickers

Recent updates have added access to an **iMessage Store** that has many applications offering fun stickers and images that you can use in your texts. The easy-to-use **App Drawer** stores many apps and images after you have downloaded them. You can navigate to this store within the **iMessage** app when texting. Follow these steps to locate these apps and stickers.

Figure 5.9: Stickers for texting

1. Tap the **App Store** icon to the left of the text message area to bring up the **App Drawer**.

2. Swipe to the left or right to locate the **App Store** icon, and then tap this icon.

3. Tap the **Visit Store** button, and the text **App Store** displays.

4. Browse the store and tap an app to download it. Apps such as **Classic Apple**, **Little Kitten**, and **Mario Brothers** stickers can be downloaded and added to messages.

 # Trick 34:

Search for Apps to Add Your Own Stickers

You can search for sticker apps by name in order to download and install, so that you have lots of stickers on your device to use for texting.

To search and download a specific sticker app:

1. Tap the **App Store** icon to the left of the text message area to bring up the **App Drawer**.

2. Swipe to the left or right to locate the **App Store** icon, and then tap this icon.

3. Tap the **Visit Store** button, and the text **App Store** displays. You can browse or tap the **magnifying glass** to search for an app by name.

4. Tap the **Get** or **Buy** button (the same way you access apps in the **App Store)**. Once you download an app, you can find it in the **App Drawer** by tapping the **App Store** icon in the text messaging area.

Trick 35:

Search App Store Animations by Category to Insert into Your Message When Texting

To search for animations for your texts by category in **iMessage**:

1. Tap the **iMessage** app, and then tap the **App Store** icon to the left of the typing area. The **App Drawer** displays.

2. Next, swipe left or right to locate the **images** page.

3. Enter a search term in the **Find Images** search bar or select from the images below.

Figure 5.10: Search animations by category

More Texting Tricks: The Texting Information Screen

When you tap the contact's circle at the top (see Figure 5.12) and then tap the **Info** icon, the **Details** screen displays. The next trick covers read receipts, which can be programmed in the **Details** menu.

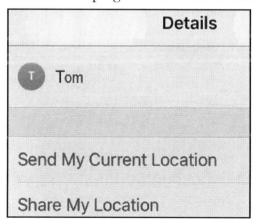

Figure 5.11: Details screen

Trick 36:

Set up Read Receipts in the Details Screen

Read receipts let you know your texts have been read by the receiver. To require a read receipt from a certain contact, perform the following steps:

Note: Having to interact with a read receipt can be annoying to those receiving your emails, so you may want to use this feature sparingly.

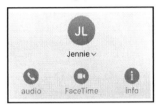

Figure 5.12: Contact's circle

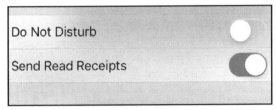

Figure 5.13: Enable Read Receipts

❑ To require a read receipt for a contact, tap the contact's circle at the top (see Figure 5.12), tap the **Info** icon at the top right, and then move the white circle to the right to enable **Send Read Receipts** (see Figure 5.13).

Figure 5.14: Message

How to Save and Delete Photos and Attachments

To **delete** an image or attachment that someone texted you, do the following:

1. From the **iMessage** screen of the contact, tap the contact's circle at the top (see Figure 5.12), and then tap the **Info** icon at the top right.

2. **Long-press** the image or attachment, and then press either **Delete** or **Delete Attachment**.

To **save** a texted image to your **Photos** app, do the following:

1. **Long-press** the image or attachment and then tap **More**.

2. At the bottom left of your screen, tap **Save Image**.

Note: The saved image will be located in your **Photos** app.

Figure 5.15: Save and delete texted images and attachments

Figure 5.16: Tap leftmost icon to access your photos when texting

 Trick 37:

Access/Send Photos When Texting

To send photos quickly when texting in iOS 12:

1. In the **iMessage** app, tap the camera icon to the left of the text box area.

2. In the **Camera** app, you can now perform the following actions:

   ☐ Take a photo with the front or rear cameras. Note that you can select **Retake** at the top to retake the photo if you don't approve. You can also add effects, edits (filters, brightness, markups) or just tap the blue arrow to send immediately (see Figure 5.17). If you want to place the photo in your text message area without sending immediately, tap **Done** at the top.

Figure 5.17: Take, retake, or add effects to photos when texting

   ☐ Tap the new **Photos** icon in the upper left (see Figure 5.16) to access your photo library.

   ☐ Add shapes, texts, filters, stickers, animations and more.

   iOS 12 has introduced extra fun effects for the camera within the **iMessage** app. When you access the **Camera** app by tapping the **Camera** icon, you can see the new **Effects** icon at the bottom left of the screen (see Figure 5.18). This allows you to access shapes, texts, filters, and stickers to add to your photos to send in text conversations.

Note: You can also insert **Animojis** and **Memojis** into your photos (See **Chapter 8** for more on animated emojis and avatars).

Figure 5.18: Effects icon

 Trick 38:

Send a Short Voice Message inside of iMessages

Sending a short voice message quickly when texting is easy:

1. Tap **iMessages**, and then tap on a new message.

2. Press down on the **microphone** to the right of the message typing area, and recording begins.

Figure 5.19: Microphone icon in the text box

3. Release the **microphone** icon when done and the recording stops.

4. To send your voice message, tap the **Up** arrow.

Note: Press the **"X"** on the left to delete the message if you decide not to send it.

Note: There is a different **microphone** icon you may see at the bottom of the keyboard when you are typing. This **microphone**, when pressed, allows you to dictate into any typing screen (text, notes, email). While the above trick creates voice clips, the handy **microphone** in the bottom keyboard area is used for dictation purposes, to convert your speech to text. Note that if you don't see a **microphone** in the keyboard, you need to go to the **Settings** app, tap **General**, tap **Keyboard**, then scroll to the bottom to locate **Enable Dictation**. Move the white circle switch to the right.

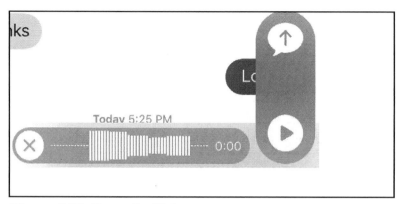

Figure 5.20: Record a Voice message

 Trick 39:

Hide Text Message Alerts From Specific People

Do you need to be notified about every new text you receive? Many texts are from people whose messages are not important to know about at the minute they arrive. You can hide alerts from designated people. Here's how!

1. Tap **iMessages,** and make sure you are in the Messages screen that displays a list of people who have texted.

2. Swipe to the left on a message from someone that you don't want alerts about the next time they text you.

3. Tap **Hide Alerts.**

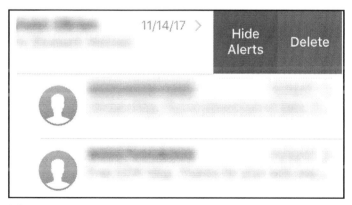

Figure 5.21: Hide text message alerts

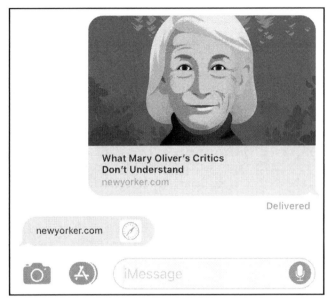

Figure 5.22: Preview links in a text

 Trick 40:

Play Videos and Web Links You Receive in iMessages and Send Them Too!

Sending or taking photos when texting is even easier!

To play a video or Web link you receive in an **iMessages** text:

❑   Tap the video or Web link you receive, and it will play in **iMessages** or take you to the link.

To send a video in an **iMessages** text:

❑   Tap **iMessages**, and then tap a new or current message. **Next**, tap the **Camera** icon to the left of the message typing area, tap **Photos**, tap the **Videos** album, and then select a video to add to your text message. Finally, press **Send**.

To send a Web link in an **iMessages** text:

❑   Tap **Safari**, and navigate to a website address. Next, **long-press** on the address at the top of the screen. Tap **Copy**, and then press the

Figure 5.23 and Figure 5.24: Copy and paste

Home button (or **swipe up from the base** on iPhone X, XS/ Max, XR models). Open **iMessage**, and create a text message. **Long-press** in the text area, tap **Paste**, and the link appears. Press **Send**.

 ## Trick 41:

Use Low Quality Image Mode When Sending Messages with Images

You can use a feature called **Low Quality Image Mode** when sending messages with image attachments. Once enabled, any photos you send through your texts will be sent in lower quality than the original. This saves a lot of room on your device, and also does not burden the recipient with an over-large image on their device.

To make this change, do the following:

1. Tap **Settings** and tap **Messages**.

2. Next, enable **Low Quality Image Mode** at the bottom of the screen (move the white circle switch to the right).

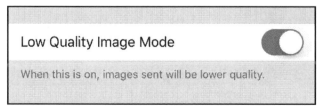

Figure 5.25: Low Quality Image mode

Trick 42:

Use Apple Pay Cash to Send Money to a Contact

Although **Apple Pay Cash** debuted in the past upgrade (iOS 11.2), there are new refinements in iOS 12. For instance, **Apple Pay Cash** notifications now make use of **3D touch** (see **Chapter 1**) so if you **long-press** a receipt notification, you can see details about the transaction without unlocking your phone.

Note: To perform this trick, you must have set up **Apple Pay Cash** in advance. To set up **Apple Pay Cash**, tap **Settings**, and then tap **Wallet & Apple Pay**. Next, tap **Add Credit or Debit Card**. Use your camera to photograph a credit card, and follow the instructions to set the card up.

❑   You and the recipient must also have a compatible device upgraded to at least iOS 11.2 or later.

❑   Two-factor authentication for your Apple ID must be set up. You can do this by signing into iCloud (see **Trick 75**).

❑   You must have enough money on your **Apple Pay Cash** card or an eligible credit or debit card in **Wallet**.

❑   You must agree to terms and conditions before you send money.

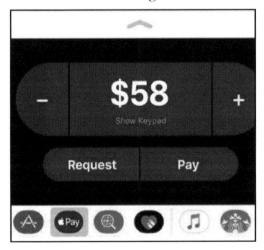

Figure 5.26: Pay or request money from a contact during texting

To use **Apple Pay** when texting:

1. Tap **iMessage** and then tap the **Apple Pay** icon in the **App Drawer** at the bottom of the screen.

2. Tap the + or - icon or tap **Show Keypad** to specify an amount.

3. Tap **Pay** to send money. Tap **Request** to request funds. You can add a message to go with the payment or request.

Updates to Apple Apps

6

There are additional iOS 12 updates to Apple apps including to the **Notes**, **Siri**, **Mail**, **Maps** apps, and more.

 Trick 43:

Collaborate with Others in Real Time Using the Notes App

You can collaborate with others in real time by inviting them to participate in a **group note** using Apple's **Notes** app.

To invite people to collaborate in a **group note**:

1. Tap the **Notes** app at the **Home** screen to launch the **Notes** app.

Note: Make sure to start at the **Folders** screen in the **Notes** app. If you don't see **Folders** at the top (as in the illustration), tap the **Back** icon (<) at the top left.

2. Tap **iCloud** and tap the **New Note** icon at the bottom right of the screen.

3. Type text in the note.

Note: If you are on a Mac, click **Share**.

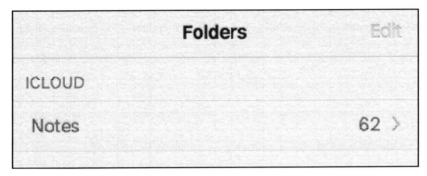

Figure 6.1: Note folder

4. Tap the **Add People** icon at the top right of the screen. Choose a method (message, email, copying link) to invite someone to collaborate (see Figure 6.2). You can add people to this note (see Figure 6.3). Once you send this invitation out, your invitees can open your note and start editing in the note at the same time as you.

Note: You and your collaborators must all update your devices to the latest iOS version. iCloud must also be set up on all devices. To make sure you are sharing a note, look for the cloud icon at the top of your note.

Figure 6.2: **Add people to the note**

Figure 6.3: **Collaborate on a note**

 **Trick 44:**

Scan a Document Using Notes

iOS 12 has added a **3D Touch** function to this feature that allows you to scan documents by long-pressing the **Notes** app icon.

To scan a document using **Notes**:

1. Tap the **Notes** app icon, and create a new note or bring up an existing note.

2. Tap the **+** icon, and then tap **Scan Documents**. (Alternately you can long-press on the **Notes** app icon, and select **Scan Document**.)

Note: Tap the screen if you don't see the + sign.

3. Arrange your document within the camera frame, and then tap the white circle (or one of the volume buttons).

4. Drag the corners of the scan to include the whole page, and then tap **Retake** or **Keep Scan**. You can add pages by positioning new documents and then tapping the white circle. When you are done, tap **Save,** and then tap **Done.**

Scan Documents

Figure 6.4: Scan a document into the Notes app

 **Trick 45:**

Pin a Note at the Top of the Notes App

Here's how to pin an important note to appear at the top of the **Notes** app so that it is always available and in view when you launch **Notes**.

1. Swipe right on the note's name that you want to pin.

Note: If you do not see the list of all of your notes, tap the link at the top left to navigate back to the list.

2. Tap the **pin** icon, and the note will stay pinned to the topmost row of the list of notes. You can unpin this note the exact same way.

Trick 46:

Create a Table in the Notes App

You can create a table in the **Notes** app. Tables let you group information in columns and rows for better organization. Here's how to set up a table in **Notes**!

1. In the **Notes** app, tap the **New Note** icon, and then tap into the note screen.

2. Tap the **Table Creation tool** at the the bottom of the screen to create a table.

Figure 6.5: Table creation tool

3. To add more columns, tap the table, then tap the **More** button that appears outside the table (the icons with three dots). The button at the top of the table adds columns; the button to the left of the table adds rows.

Figure 6.6: More dots

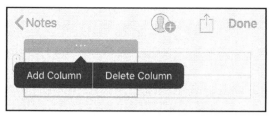

Figure 6.7: Add or delete column

4. Tap the **Add** or **Delete Column** (or **Row**) selection to further customize your table.

 Trick 47:

Add a Sketch to a Note in the Notes App

Another feature allows you to add a drawing to a note in the **Notes** app. You can also use the pencil to create a handwritten message, and this message will become immediately searchable in the future. Here's how!

1. Tap the **New Note** icon, and then tap into the note's screen.

2. Tap the **plus sign** (+) at the the bottom, and then tap **Add Sketch**. Use the drawing tools at the bottom to create a sketch or a handwritten message.

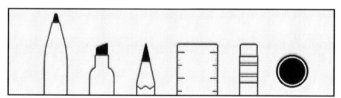

Figure 6.8: Sketch tools in the Notes app

Other New Notes Features

❑ **Add Notes to Control Center** – Adding the **Notes** control to **Control Center** lets you access **Notes** from the **Lock** screen. See **Chapter 2** to learn how to add a control.

❑ **Take a Photo or Video or Access Your Photos** – Press the **+** icon, and then tap either of these choices.

❑ **Tap the Apple Pencil on Your iPad** –Tap the Apple **Pencil** on an iPad's **Lock** screen, and the **Notes** app will open right away.

Trick 48:

Save time by Filtering Emails in Apple Mail To View Only Unread Messages

It's easy to quickly filter your emails in Apple **Mail** so that you only see unread messages.

To do so:

1. Launch Apple's **Mail** app, and tap your email provider.

2. Tap the circular icon at the bottom left of the screen. It becomes filled with blue (instead of just outlined in blue) and you'll see a message that displays **Filtered by: Unread**. Tap the icon again to turn the filter off.

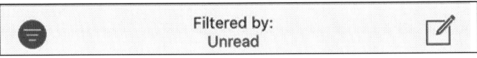

Figure 6.9: Filter unread messages

 ## Trick 49:

Use the "Fast Unsubscribe" Feature

Any emails with unsubscribe possibilities display this link at the **top of each message**, so you can easily tap this link to unsubscribe.

It really makes it easy to unsubscribe instead of having to page down, and look for a tiny unsubscribe link.

This message is from a mailing list.
Unsubscribe

Figure 6.10: Easily unsubscribe from a mailing list

Apple Safari Updates

iOS 12 has concentrated on security features for **Safari**, making it hard for sites to track you without your permission. Apple has also disabled features that let advertisers track you and analyze your movements. These updates are important, but more subtle than those in the last update, which introduced the ability to open two windows at the same time, to close your open tabs all at once, to drag and drop between windows, and to customize the iPad's dock. Here are some tricks to help you to make the most of using **Safari**.

Trick 50:

Open up Two Safari Windows at the Same Time on Your iPad

It is very helpful to be able to open two windows at the same time on your iPad. To do this in **Safari**, tap and hold on a link, and then select **Open in Split View**. Finally, drag a tab to the left or right side of the screen. To restore a normal full screen, simply drag the tab in the middle back to either side. **Split View** also allows you to switch between two apps, and you can drag notes, photos, and more between different apps.

 # Trick 51:

Drag Apps/MultiTasking the New iPad Dock

New features came with past updates for the iPad, including the addition of a customizable dock. You can move icons to/from the dock. Here's how!

1. Tap **Safari,** then swipe up from the iPad's bottom frame to see the dock.

2. In the newly-displayed dock, press and hold the **Messages** icon and drag it to the side of the screen. It will open in a small window for you to read/send messages without exiting **Safari**. Drag a photo over the **Notes** app, keeping your finger pressed, and **Notes** will let you select a note. You can also long-press to see files in the **Files** app (Fig. 6.11).

Figure 6.11: Drag apps into the dock and preview files in the Files app

Close 90 Tabs

Figure 6.12: Clear all tabs

 Trick 52:

Clear Safari Tabs All At Once

On an iPad, **long-press** the **Tab View** icon, and a menu displays the **Close Tabs** option (see Figure 6.12 above). On the iPhone, tap the **Tab View** icon, and then **long-press** on **Done**, in order to view the **Close Tabs** option.

 Trick 53:

Create a PDF in Safari

In Safari, you can create a **PDF** (Portable Document Format) version of a Web page for the purpose of sharing, printing, or more. A **PDF** is a file format that provides an image of text/graphics and looks like a printed document and can be viewed, printed, and more. The IRS uses **PDF** forms to preserve the formatting of their documents. You can email a **PDF** document to another person and it will display the same way on his/her screen as it looks on yours, including fonts, margins, etc. To convert a Web page to a **PDF**:

1. From the **Home** screen, tap **Safari**, and then navigate to a Web page article that you would like to convert to a **PDF**.

2. Tap the **Share** icon, and then swipe left until you see **Create PDF**.

   Note: If the **Create PDF** choice is too far to the right in the line of icons, you can **long-press** this icon and drag it to the left to relocate it for the future. Many people prefer to also relocate the **Print** icon so that it is closer to the first set of icons that appear when you tap **Share**.

3. Tap **Create PDF**, and a **PDF** displays on-screen.

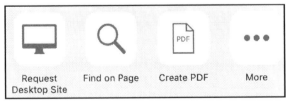

Figure 6.13: Create a PDF

Figure 6.14: Mark up the PDF

Notes:

You can also convert documents and notes to a **PDF** using the **Share** icon as outlined in this trick.

You can add annotations to the **PDF** immediately after it is created. A little marker tip icon displays at the top right.

When you click this icon, it brings up different drawing tools that display at the bottom.

The **PDF** tools include tools to add text use a text box, magnify an area of text, add your signature, and more.

When you have completed your mark-up, you must tap **Done** at the top left of the screen.

5. To save the **PDF**, tap the **Share** button again, and then tap **Save File To**. Specific locations display, e.g. apps or folders in the **Files** app (see Chapter 3) like **iCloud Drive** which also can include cloud storage services such as Dropbox. You can also save the attachment to an app or location on your iPhone by selecting **On My iPhone**.

6. Tap **Add** at the upper right, and then tap **Done**.

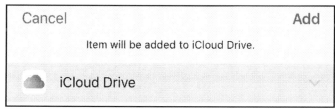

Figure 6.15: Add the PDF to a selected location

Trick 54:

Access Flight Information ASAP in Safari

Many of us use apps to find out flight information, but it is easier to find flight information by just typing the flight number in the address bar (also called **Smart Search** bar). Here's how!

1. Tap **Safari**, and then type the airline and flight number in the top **Smart Search** bar until the information appears under **Flights**.

Figure 6.16: Safari smart search bar

2. Tap the flight information, and you can view the flight path, and other important details such as gate number, status, and more.

Figure 6.17: Flight tracking information

Trick 55:

Read Website Articles Later, Offline

In today's fast-paced life, there is rarely enough time to read the full text of online articles. However, a little-known trick allows these articles to be saved to your device(s), and read later. Excellent opportunities to read these articles include when you are on a plane, in traffic, in a long line at the bank or at the grocery store. To save an article to read it later:

Note: Before beginning this trick, you must navigate to **Settings > Safari> Reading List**, and then enable **Automatically Save Offline**.

1. Tap **Safari**, and then navigate to a news or entertainment site that features different articles.

2. Tap one of the articles, and when it fully loads onto your screen, tap the **Share** icon.

Figure 6.18: Share and Bookmark icons

3. Tap the **Add to Reading List** icon, and your article will be saved to your device.

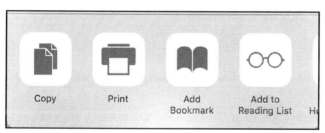

Figure 6.19: Add to Reading List icon

4. To retrieve your article, tap the **Bookmark** icon (see Figure 6.18), and then tap the middle area showing the "glasses" icon to find the article(s) you have saved (see Figure 6.20).

5. Tap each article to read it. To delete an article, you must swipe to the left on the article name, and then tap **Delete**.

6. Tap **Done** when you want to exit the **Bookmark/Reading List** screen.

Figure 6.20: Reading List

Siri App Updates

The **Siri** app has always been designed to be a personal assistant, and "her" abilities have been increased in iOS 12. She sounds more human and can now tell you who is calling, translate into different languages, set up a ride with Uber or Lyft, search through your photos, work with non-Apple apps, and accept pre-fabricated shortcuts (see **Trick 96**)!

> **Note**: To find people (**Trick 58**), you may have to first identify them manually in the **People** folder (**see Chapter 4** to learn how to identify people in **Photos**).

Figure 6.21: Siri announces callers

 # Trick 56:

Set Up Siri to Tell You Who is Calling

You can set up **Siri** to tell you who is calling you. You can set this to occur all the time or decide to have Siri only alert you in certain situations, such as when you are connected via **CarPlay stereo** or while using headphones.

To enable this feature, do the following:

1. Tap **Settings**, tap **iPhone**, and enable **Announce Calls**.

2. Select **Always**, **Never**, **Headphones Only**, or **Headphones & Car**.

Trick 57:

Communicate With Siri Via Text

Sometimes it isn't convenient to use your voice to talk to Siri, such as in a public place. Instead, you can type commands and questions. Here's how!

1. Tap **Settings**, tap **General**, and then tap **Accessibility**.

2. Enable **Type to Siri**.

Once this new feature is enabled, **long-pressing** the **Home** button (or the **On/Off** button on the right side of the iPhone X, XS/Max, XR models) brings up a keyboard in the **Siri** screen. Type in questions/commands and you are good to go! Note that you must reverse this procedure to turn off this feature.

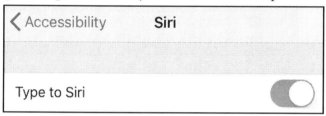

Figure 6.22: Type to Siri feature

 # Trick 58:

Ask Siri to Search Your Photos

If **Siri** is enabled in **Settings** (tap **Settings**, tap **Siri & Search**, and make sure **Siri** is enabled), and you have previously identified people in the Photos app (see **Chapter 4**), then you can simply hold the **Home** button (or the **On/Off** side button on the iPhone 10/X, XS/Max, XR models), and tell **Siri** to show you photos of a specific person, place, or thing.

Figure 6.23: Search photos with Siri

Trick 59:

Let Siri Be Your Translator

Siri can translate from American English to French, German, Italian, Spanish, & Mandarin. More languages are on the way. Here's how to ask!

1. Activate **Siri** by pressing the **Home** button (or the **On/Off** side button on the iPhone 10/X, XS/Max, XR models).

2. Say this phrase to Siri: **"Translate where is the car to Spanish"**. You can also phrase the command as **"How do you say where is the train station in German"**.

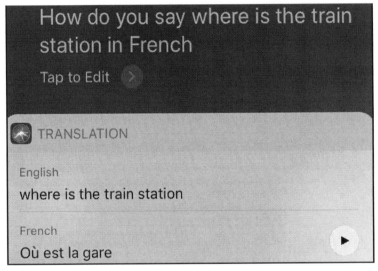

Figure 6.24: Ask Siri to translate

 ## Trick 60:

Enlist Siri to Work with Ride Apps Like Uber & Lyft

Note: To ask **Siri** to work with these third-party apps, you must first download these apps from the **App Store** and then install them. In addition, you must turn on the setting that allows **Siri** to work with a supported third-party app. To do so, tap **Settings**, tap **Siri**, tap **App Support** and then enable some or all of the apps listed.

Figure 6.25: Enable ride app support in Settings > Siri

Perform these actions to use Siri to work with **Uber** and **Lyft** apps.

1. **Long-press** the **Home** button (or the **On/Off** side button on the iPhone 10/X, XS/Max, XR models) to access **Siri**.

2. Say **"Siri, book me a ride with Lyft."** Siri works with this app, and give you the time and other details. You can then either order the ride at that time or schedule when and where to be picked up.

Figure 6.26: Schedule a Lyft ride with Siri

 Trick 61:

Change the Wallpaper on Your Home Screen

Each update introduces new wallpaper, and iOS 12 is no exception. If you update your operating system to iOS 12, and would like to change the wallpaper on your **Home** (or **Lock**) screen, follow these instructions.

1. From the **Home** screen, tap **Settings**, and then tap **Wallpaper**.

2. Tap **Choose New Wallpaper**, select a wallpaper showing custom backgrounds (or access one of your own photos), and then select **Set Home screen** (or **Lock** screen).

Phone and Contacts App Updates

There are some new helpful updates to your **Phone** and **Contacts** apps to explore in the following tricks.

 # Trick 62:

Download the HiYa app to Set Up Call Blocking/Notifications

The **HiYa** app can be downloaded from the **App Store**. Once you have downloaded it and set it up, perform the following steps to integrate it into Apple settings.

1. Tap **Settings**, and then tap **Phone**.

2. Tap **Call Block & Identification**.

3. Enable **HiYa** by moving the white circle switch to the right, and you will begin to get important information about your calls. Your device will also begin to block the errant calls.

Figure 6.27: Research any number in HiYa

Note: To block callers in Apple's **Phone** app, simply tap the **Phone** app, tap **Recents** on the bottom menu bar, tap the **Info** icon to the right of any number, and then scroll down to the bottom in the next screen. Next tap **Block This Caller**.

Trick 63:

Set Priorities in How You Want to Communicate With Your Contacts

You can now set your preferred communication method for each of your contacts by different categories such as call, message, or mail. You may prefer to stick to email for one person, while being open to any other ways of communication with another person. To set the priority, perform the following steps:

1. Tap the **Phone** app, and then tap **Favorites** in the bottom menu bar.

2. Tap the **+** icon in the top let corner.

3. Add a contact by tapping it.

4. Choose between **Message**, **Call**, **Video**, or **Mail**. To locate a different email or phone number if there is more than one, tap the down arrow to the right of the contact. Your contact displays in your **Favorites** list.

Figure 6.28: Prioritize your communication with contacts

Note: You can change the position of a **Favorite** by tapping **Edit** in the upper-right corner. You can also add these contact **Favorites** as one of your widgets on the **Lock** screen.

Apple Maps

Some wonderful features have come along in recent updates for the Apple **Maps** app, including mapping of indoor malls/airports, parking space directions, ways to avoid freeways and/or toll roads! In addition, Apple **Maps** has been integrated in the **Calendar** app so when you enter an event into **Calendar**, map locations are suggested. iOS 12 has introduced a new **Maps** engine that displays more detailed maps complete with public landmarks, parks, and greenery. San Francisco was the first city to reflect this ultra-detailed view, and other cities will be updated similarly in the next year.

 Trick 64:

Ask Siri To Remind You of Your Car's Location

Note: This trick only works if **Show Parked Location** is enabled in **Settings**. To make sure this feature is enabled, tap **Settings**, then **Maps**, and make sure **Show Parked Location** is enabled (as shown in Figure 6.29). In addition, you must have **Bluetooth** or **CarPlay stereo** enabled in your car (although alternate instructions follow if you don't have these car features).

1. Press and hold the **Home** button to launch **Siri** (or the **On/Off** side button on the iPhone 10/X, XS/Max, XR models). You can also say "**Hey Siri**" if that has been enabled in your **Settings** app under Settings > **Siri & Search**).

Show Parked Location

Your parked car will be shown on the map if your location can be determined when parking. A connection to your car's Bluetooth or CarPlay stereo is required.

Figure 6.29: Show parked location enabled in Settings > Maps

2. Say the following words to **Siri**: "**Where did I park?**"

Siri displays your parked location within a map, and also show you how far away in measurements, such as feet, miles, etc.

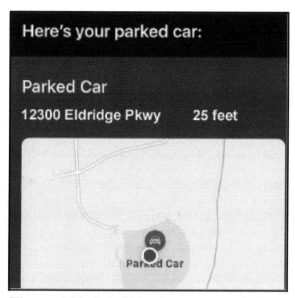

Figure 6.30: Ask Siri where you parked

As long as you have **Bluetooth or CarPlay** stereo in your car, this features works automatically.

If you do not have **Bluetooth or CarPlay** stereo in your car, you can ask **Siri** to mark any location where you stop in order to find your car later. You can find this option in the **Maps** program as detailed in the following sections.

Mark Your Location With 3D Touch

To manually mark your location using **3D Touch**:

1. **Long-press** the **Maps** app icon on your **Home** screen.

2. Tap **Mark My Location.** The **Maps** app opens, and a pin will be set at your location. It will also be labeled as "marked location," a term that can be searched later on in **Maps**.

Mark Your Location Manually

To manually mark your location on phones without 3D Touch:

1. Tap the **Maps** app from the **Home** screen.

2. Tap the **Location** arrow to find your current location.

3. Tap the **Info** icon, and then tap **Mark My Location.** A pin will mark your current location.

Find a Marked Location

Note: These directions only work if you manually created the **Marked Location** item when you parked. Once it is created, it can be searched for.

To find your marked location once it has been automatically set:

1. Tap the **Maps** app, and then tap the **Search** bar at the bottom of the screen.

2. Type **Marked Location**, and your location displays.

3. Tap **Directions** button, tap the **Walk** icon at the bottom of the screen, and then tap **Go** to get walking directions to your car.

 Trick 65:

Take Interactive City Tours with Maps' Flyover Feature

You can take advantage of the updated **Flyover** feature and interact with a 3D augmented-reality video of cities around the world. Here's how!

Note: Flyover is not interactive in models earlier than the 6S.

1. From the **Home** screen, tap the **Maps** icon and then type a well-known city like New York City, Florence, London, Paris etc., and then tap the **Flyover Tour** button.

2. Tilt and rotate your device to move through the city. It will move forward as you walk. Pinch and zoom to navigate around each city for a fully immersive experience.

Figure 6.31: Empire State Building

Trick 66:

Get Hourly Weather Reports from Apple Maps (select iPhone models only)

Note: You must have a device that supports **3D Touch**.

You can see weather **by the hour** when you are in the **Maps** app.

To enable this feature, perform the following steps:

1. Tap **Maps**, and look for the current temperature unit in the bottom-right corner.

2. **Long-press** on the temperature, and the weather-by-hour pop-up displays.

Note: If you continue to long-press on the temperature unit, the weather app displays.

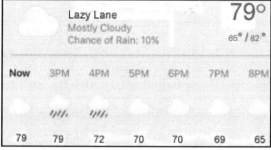

Figure 6.32: Get hourly weather in Maps

 ## Trick 67:

Avoid Tolls (and Highways) Along Your Route

You can choose to avoid toll roads using **Maps**. To enable this setting, go to **Settings**, **Maps**, and then tap **Driving & Navigation**. Enable **Avoid Tolls** (and **Highways** if desired). With this setting on, **Maps** will automatically give you a **no-toll-roads** route. Simply get directions as you normally would by typing in your destination and tapping **Directions**. Apple **Maps** displays the non-toll route.

Figure 6.33: Avoid tolls and highways

Other New Maps Features

Here are a few more **Maps** features that you should also try.

☐ **3D Maps** – Type in a location in **Maps**, and then use two fingers to swipe up the screen. After a brief time period, it will show the map in 3D style. To restore the normal screen, you can tap back on 2D in the icon area at the top right.

☐ **Lane Guidance/Speed Limits** – **Maps** now shows which lane you should be in when turning and it also displays the speed limit.

☐ **Mapped Indoor Airports/Malls** – Selected indoor spaces are now mapped. Just launch **Maps** at any major city's airport to try it out!

Figure 6.34: 3D map view

Miscellaneous Updates & Extra Tricks

7

Apple Apps

Past updates brought an enhanced level of flexibility to Apple apps. We can delete some Apple apps we don't need, move apps around the screen in groups, and much more.

 ## Trick 68:

Delete Apple Apps You Don't Want

In past upgrades, users gained the ability to delete some unwanted Apple apps, and to reinstall them from the **App Store** app if they should be needed in the future.

□   To delete an Apple app, press lightly on the app until all apps wiggle, tap the "**X**" on the upper left side of the app, and then confirm the deletion.

Figure 7.1: Delete Apple apps

Tip: If your phone has **3D Touch**, and you are having a hard time getting the icons to wiggle, just rest your finger lightly. This should cause all icons to wiggle.

 ## Trick 69:

Move Apps Around the Screen in Groups

We used to have to move apps around one at a time, but recent updates have given us the ability to move apps in groups. Here's how!

1. From the **Home** screen, press down (lightly on devices with **3D Touch**) on one app until all apps start to wiggle.

2. Tap one or more icons without letting go of the first one, and they will join the first app in a cluster. A red badge displays the numerical count of the clustered apps. Next, move the app icons to a new location, and release. The entire group will move to the new location.

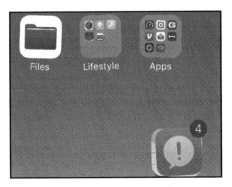

Figures 7.2: Move apps in groups

 ## Trick 70:

Play a Sound to Find Your AirPods

The **Find My iPhone** app allows you to find your lost wireless Apple AirPods by playing a sound that you can activate in this app. Here's how!

Note: For this trick to work, your AirPods must be connected via Bluetooth, and they need to be nearby.

1. Locate and then tap the **Find My iPhone** app. If your AirPods are connected to the iPhone, they will appear in the list of devices.

2. Tap **AirPods**, and then tap **Actions**.

3. Next, tap **Play Sound**. (To stop the sound, tap **Stop Playing**.)

Note: If your AirPods are in their case, they will not play a sound.

Note: If your AirPods have died, a sound won't be played, but their last location displays in the app on the map.

Figure 7.3: Find AirPods

 ## Trick 71:

Free Up Storage By Offloading Apps

Recent upgrades offered new ways of freeing up storage, one of which is the practice of offloading apps. This deletes an app but keeps its data in case you want to it download it again in the future. To offload an app:

1. Tap **Settings**, tap **General**, and then tap **iPhone Storage**.

2. Tap one of the apps that appears in the list and which you don't use much, and then tap **Offload App**.

3. Tap **Offload App** again to confirm this choice. The app will be deleted but if you want to use it in the future, you can download it again and your past data will appear in the app.

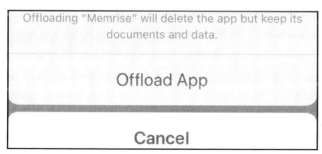

Figure 7.4: Offload an app

Trick 72:

Try More Tricks to Free Up Device Storage

Now you can review and delete large attachments that people sent you in texts to free up your iPhone/iPad data storage capability. In addition, you can program your devices to auto delete old messages and attachments. Here's how!

1. Tap **Settings**, tap **General**, and then tap **iPhone Storage**.

2. Tap **Review Large Attachments** to view all the extra attachments (photos, files) that are taking up space on your device within the **iMessage** app.

   ❑ If you know that you want to delete the attachment, swipe to the left and then tap **Delete**.

   ❑ If you want to review, email, print etc, tap each attachment and then tap the **Share** icon. Tap **Done** when you are finished.

Note: In the same menu, you can enable the **auto-delete** feature to delete messages and attachments that were sent or received over a year ago.

 Trick 73:

Use SOS to Call for Emergency Help

On your iPhone, if you press the **On/Off** button rapidly five times in a row, emergency services will be called. This action also disables the **Touch ID** fingerprint reader on models with **Touch ID**.

Note: On the iPhone X and other select models, hold the **On/Off** button plus one of the volume buttons at the same time to initiate **Emergency SOS**.

To set up emergency services contacts, perform the following steps:

1. Tap **Settings**, and then tap **Emergency SOS**.

2. In this menu, enable the **Auto Call** setting so emergency services will be contacted.

3. Tap the **Set up Emergency Contacts in Health** link. By adding one or more of your contacts to the **Medical ID** section of the **Apple Health** app, you will ensure contacts receive the SOS and your current location.

You can also set up specified contacts. After an emergency call ends, your device alerts your contacts with a text message, unless you choose to cancel. Your device sends them your current location, and, for a period of time after you enter **SO S** mode, it sends your contacts updates when your location changes. Note that iOS 12 now automatically shares emergency locations with 911.

To set up **SOS** contacts:

1. Tap **Settings**, tap **Emergency SOS**, and then tap **Set up Emergency Contacts** in Health.

   Note: You can also tap the **Health** app from the **Home** screen, and tap the **Medical ID** tab.

2. Tap **Edit**, then scroll to **Emergency Contacts**.

3. Tap the **plus** sign to add an emergency contact.

4. Tap a contact, add their relationship to you, and then tap **Done**.

Figure 7.5: Emergency SOS menu

Trick 74:

Join Friends/Family Network with Wi-Fi Sharing

When visiting friends or family, you might want to get on their Wi-Fi network. In the past, you needed to find out their password. Now all you need to do is make sure your device and your relative or friend's device has the most recent update installed on both devices to join effortlessly. Here's how!

1. Tap **Settings**, and then tap **Wi-Fi**.

2. Tap your friend or relative's network, and the password screen will appear.

3. Make sure your device is near the other device belonging to your friend or family member. A pop-up menu displays that lets the other person know that your device is trying to join the network. Your friend or relative must then tap **Share Password** to send the Wi-Fi password to your phone. After a short delay, the iPhone password field will fill in on your device and it will connect to the new network.

Figure 7.6: Wi-Fi password sharing

Trick 75:

Access Your Backed-Up Photos/Files in iCloud From Your Mobile Device

On your laptop or desktop computer, you can type "iCloud.com" into the address bar of your browser, and reach the iCloud sign-in page. From there, all you need to do is type in your Apple ID and password, click the arrow, and then find your backed up photos, files, notes, and more. However, on your iPhone/iPad, if you try the same procedure in Safari (or another browser), you will not reach the same page.

Here's how to access your iCloud backed-up files from your mobile devices.

1. On your iPad/iPhone, tap **Safari** (or another browser) and then type **iCloud.com** in the top bar of the browser.

2. Ignore the screen that displays, and instead, tap the **Share** icon, and then tap **Request Desktop Site**. The "iCloud.com" sign-on page displays.

Note: You may have to swipe left to slide the icons to find the **Request Desktop Site** selection. Yet the iCloud page that displays is not as easy to navigate on an iPhone as compared to an iPad or laptop. However, it is a handy trick to know when you need to access your files from your mobile device. Note that you can view and also download/delete your iCloud files using computers/mobile devices.

Figure 7.7: Request Desktop site

Trick 76:

Try Out the Easy Shut Down Feature

If your power button is not functioning, or you prefer an easier solution than pressing the power button to turn off your device, try this new feature that allows you to shut down your iPhone through the **Settings** app. Here's how!

1. Tap **Settings**, and then tap **General**.

2. Tap **Shut Down**. The new screen displays the normal **Slide To Power Off** message.

‹ Settings	**General**
iTunes Wi-Fi Sync	
VPN	Not Connected
Regulatory	
Reset	
Shut Down	

Figure 7.8: iPhone Shut Down feature

 Trick 77:

Turn Off Auto-Brightness To Boost Battery

One way to help extend battery life is to turn off the new Auto-Brightness feature, which brightens or dims your screen based on the lighting conditions around you. It's much better to manually set brightness. Here's how!

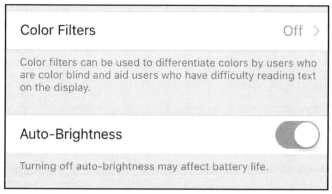

Figure 7.9: Auto-Brightness setting

1. Tap **Settings**, tap **General**, and then tap **Accessibility**.

2. Tap **Display Accommodations**.

3. Disable the **Auto-Brightness** switch (if it is already enabled) by dragging it to the left.

Note: If you decide to keep this feature on, note that you can still manually adjust brightness in **Control Center** with **Auto-Brightness** enabled.

 Trick 78:

Reverse Screen Color with Smart Invert

For those who like the crisp clarity of a black screen with white text, there is a new feature that accomplishes this "reverse-out" without ruining images or other media. To try this mode out, follow the steps below.

1. Tap **Settings**, tap **General**, and then tap **Accessibility**.

2. Tap **Display Accommodations**, and then tap **Invert Colors**.

3. Enable the **Smart Invert** switch by dragging it to the right. To disable this feature, drag the switch to the left.

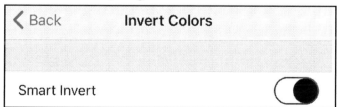

Figure 7.10: Reverse screen color

Trick 79:

Access the Left and Right Keyboards

So many of us find ourselves typing messages and emails one-handed, and having to use our thumb to tap each letter. Recent upgrades have made this mode of typing much easier by introducing a left and right keyboard option. Each one, when selected, appears on either the left or right of your screen instead of the central area. The normal keyboard can be easily restored, so this additional feature can be a valuable asset if you are holding groceries and trying to respond to a text! To access the new keyboards, follow these steps.

1. Tap **iMessage** (or an email or similar text program) and then **long-press** the emoji/globe icon at the bottom-left of the keyboard.

2. Tap the left or right keyboard icon that displays on-screen. The keyboard slides to the left or to the right side.

Note: To restore the normal centered keyboard, simply tap the arrow on the far right or the far left of the screen.

Figure 7.11: Left and right keyboard

 # Trick 80:

Check Your Battery Usage and Health

Many people noticed battery drain after upgrading to the iOS 11 version of the operating system. In response, Apple instituted a program to replace batteries in older phones for $29.00. Older iPhones, such as 6 and earlier, now run even faster than they ever did after downloading iOS 12 after also replacing the battery. In addition, recent updates brought a new feature that allows you to check battery health (which has been further refined in iOS 12) as described in then next trick.

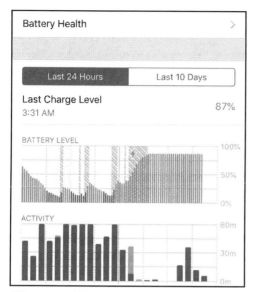

Figure 7.12: Battery info in graphs

To view information about your battery, tap **Settings**, and then tap **Battery**. iOS 12 has enhanced the readouts about both your battery's charge level and activity with colorful graphs showing information over a period of the last 24 hours or for the last 10 days. This screen also shows the proportion of your battery's usage by each app.

To further check battery health, tap **Battery Health** at the top. There are two settings: **Maximum Capacity,** which tells you the state of your current battery (and if it should be replaced) and **Peak Performance Capability** which lets you know if your battery can support normal peak performance.

Other Ways to Boost Battery Performance

Past upgrades had a lot of issues, but one of the most problematic was constant battery drain. Here are strategies to prevent poor performance.

- ❏ **Turn off the background refreshing of apps** – Tap **Settings**, tap **General**, tap **Background App Refresh** twice, and tap **Off** to prevent battery drain from apps refreshing in the background.

- ❏ **Check Battery Usage in Settings** – Tap **Settings**, and then tap **Battery** to see which apps are using the most battery power.

- ❏ **Use Low Power Mode (select models only)** – Tap this icon in **Control Center** when the battery is low and you can't charge your device.

❑ **Change Facebook and Twitter settings** – You may have noticed when you went to check your battery usage in **Settings** that these programs drain the battery. Some people prefer to access these apps using **Safari** instead of having to deal with the memory-hogging, battery-draining properties of these apps. Playing videos automatically is one feature in both apps that contributes to battery drain. You can change this feature in these apps as follows:

❑ **Facebook** – From the **Menu**, tap **Settings**, tap **Account Settings**, tap **Videos and Photos**, tap **Autoplay**, and then tap **Never Autoplay Videos**.

❑ **Twitter** – From your **Profile** area, tap **Settings and privacy**, tap **Data usage**, tap **Video autoplay**, and then tap **Select Never**.

❑ **Turn off notifications** – Tap **Settings**, and then tap **Notifications** to view all of the apps that have notifications on. You can turn off all unnecessary notifications here.

❑ **Make sure Location Services apps are set to Never** (or **While Using** if the app is location-dependent) – Tap **Settings**, tap **Privacy**, tap **Location Services**, and then tap each app that displays to make sure the **Never** selection is checked. If your app is location-dependent, select **While Using**. By doing this, you ensure that apps are not constantly updating your locations in the background, which drains the battery, and also invades your privacy.

❑ **Turn off sending data to Apple** – Tap **Settings**, tap **Privacy**, tap **Analytics**, and then turn off **Share iPhone Analytics** to save battery power.

❑ **Disable Fitness Tracking** – Tap **Settings**, tap **Privacy**, tap **Motion & Fitness**, and turn off **Fitness Tracking**.

❑ **Turn off System Services** – Tap **Settings**, tap **Privacy**, tap **Location Services**, tap **System Services**, and turn off everything but **Find My iPhone, Emergency SOS** (unless you don't need it) and **Compass Calibration** (if you like to use the handy **Compass** app).

Trick 81:

Use Focus Lock in Magnifier

When **Magnifier** is launched (see **Chapter 1** for information on how to launch **Magnifier**), you may still need better visibility in low-light situations. One feature that augments magnification in low light is called **Focus Lock**, which is the lock tool at the bottom. This feature allows you to manually select one screen area to focus on, instead of letting the device continually auto focus. Here's how to use it.

1. Launch the **Magnifier**, and tap the **Flashlight** (lightning bolt) icon to get more light on the object of magnification.

2. Orient your device so that you get a clear focus, and then tap the **Focus Lock** icon. This locks the focus for you. Tap the lock icon again to turn off **Focus Lock**.

Figure 7.13: Magnification Slider, Flashlight, Focus Lock, & Freeze Frame icons

 Trick 82:

Use Freeze Frame in Magnifier

You can freeze a magnified image on the screen, and then be able to zoom in and out on the image. Here's how!

1. Launch the **Magnifier**, then orient your device so that you have a magnified image on your screen.

2. Tap the **Freeze Frame** icon (white circle in the bottom center) so that the image freezes on the screen.

3. Move the magnification slider (the topmost tool) to zoom in and out on the still image, so that you can display the image at optimum magnification. Note that you need to tap the circle again (which displays as a gray color) to release the freeze frame feature when done.

 Trick 83:

Set Up "Do Not Disturb While Driving"

Apple has enabled users to set up how to respond to texts and phone calls while driving. You can change how this feature launches, and you can customize your replies. Here's how!

1. Tap **Settings**, tap **Do Not Disturb**, and then scroll down and tap **Activate**.

2. Tap either **Automatically** (which turns this feature on based on motion sensors that tell the software that you are driving), **When Connected to Car Bluetooth** (which launches this feature when a Bluetooth connection is active) or **Manually** (by selecting the icon in **Control Center)**.

3. Next, tap the **Do Not Disturb** link at the top left of the screen to go back to the previous menu.

4. Tap **Auto-Reply** to customize the existing message designated to be sent to people who call or text you while you are driving.

Note: You can also select **Auto-Reply To** in the **Do Not Disturb** menu to automatically reply to either recent callers/texters, to those listed in your **Phone** app as **Favorites,** or to all of your contacts.

Figure 7.14: Do Not Disturb While Driving

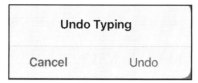

Figure 7.15: Undo accidental deletions

 Trick 84:

Shake Your Device to Undo Accidental Deletions

This trick has been around for many years, but a lot of people are unaware of it. The ability to immediately undo an accidental deletion can stop a lot of stress when you accidentally lose important text. Here's how!

Note: This trick must be performed immediately after a deletion, and it also may not work in some apps.

1. Bring up the **Notes** app.

2. Type in some text.

3. Highlight the text, tap a key, and then shake your device. The **Undo Typing** dialog box displays.

4. Tap **Undo**, and the text returns. Tap away from the highlighted text in the white space to remove the highlight so as not to erase it again!

 Trick 85:

Turn Off Transcribed Voicemails (iPhone 6S phones or later and Select Carriers Only)

Your iPhone currently transcribes voicemails. It may take a minute or two, but when it is complete, you can tap the voicemail to see the transcription. This feature requires iOS 10/11/12, an iPhone 6S or later, a carrier that supports Visual Voicemail, and one that delivers an English-only transcription. At this time, there is no way to turn off this feature if you find it annoying, however, you might try the following workaround.

1. From the **Home** screen, tap **Settings**, tap **Siri & Search**, and then tap **Language**.

2. Change the language to Australian English or Indian English (if it doesn't work, choose another variation of English but not Canadian English, since that is set up for transcription). If it works, you should see **Transcription Unavailable**

iOS 12 Key Updates & Tricks

8

There are so many new exciting features in the iOS 12 update that some of the most important ones have been included in this chapter.

 ## Trick 86:

Learn to Use the New Measure App

There have been other third-party apps in the past which turned your device into a measuring instrument, but with the newest update, Apple took over the measuring-app space. The new **Measure** app allows you to measure everything from boxes, paintings, tables, walls, and other objects in a very simple fashion that involves using just a few taps. Here's how!

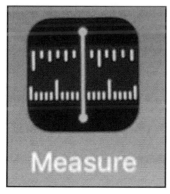

Figure 8.1: The Measure app

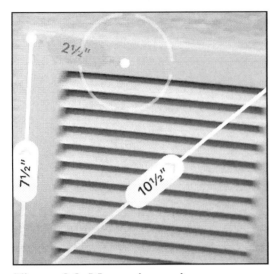

Figure 8.2: Measuring points

1. From the **Home** screen, tap the **Measure** app.

Note: You will be prompted to move your device before beginning. A white circle enclosing a white dot displays on the screen. This circle is very important for the measuring process.

2. Point your device to where you want to begin, line up the white dot there, and then tap the + button on the bottom to place the first point.

3. Move your device towards the second point. A line emerges from the first point. When you reach the second point, tap the + sign to anchor your second point, and the measurement displays.

Note: If the item is rectangular, a yellow box may show up around it. You can just tap on the rectangle to get the full measurement dimensions.

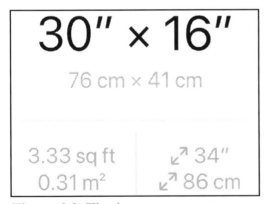

Figure 8.3: Final measurements

4. Once the measurement displays on-screen, long-press this measurement result to display the measurements in feet, inches, or centimeters.

Note: To take a photo of the finished measurement, tap the white circle at the bottom right corner.

Note: If you make a mistake while measuring, tap the **Undo** icon in the top left-hand corner to undo the most recent point. You can also start over again and delete the measurement by tapping the **Clear** button at the top right.

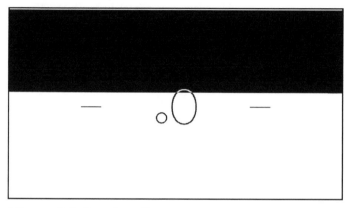

Figure 8.4: Level tool

 Trick 87:

Learn to Use the Level Tool

The **Level** tool once could be found within the **Compass** app, and it was one of the best-kept secrets in earlier versions. Now, with the advent of iOS 12, this tool has been moved into the **Measure** app, where it is certain to get more attention! Here's how to access and use the **Level** tool.

1. From the **Home** screen, tap the **Measure** app to open it.

2. Tap the **Level** tab at the bottom right of the screen.

3. Place your device on a table or any other edge, and note the screen dimensions, which should display "0" if the sides are even.

Understanding the Screen Time Feature

You may not realize how much time you spend on your iPhone and iPad until you see some kind of detailed accounting. A new feature called **Screen Time** in iOS 12 lets you know how much time you spend on your device, and how much time you spend on individual apps. This feature also displays a weekly summary of your habits, and lets you set time limits for using any of your apps, which is a great feature for those with young children. When you first access **Screen Time**, you will be asked if this is your device or your child's device. You can then follow the on-screen instructions to set up your child's device. Once you set time limits, you will be automatically notified when time runs out. To access **Screen Time**, tap **Settings**, and then tap **Screen Time**.

> **Note: Screen Time** can be added as a widget on the **Lock** screen. See **Chapter 2** for instructions on how to add a widget to the **Lock** screen.

- ❑ **See Your Screen Time** – In **Settings** > **Screen Time**, tap the name of your device that displays at the top to analyze your recent activity. Next, tap **Today** or **Last 7 Days** at the time to see the time spent on your device, your most used apps, your "pickups" (how often you picked up the device), and your notifications/messages received during the two above-mentioned time periods.

- ❑ **Set Up Downtime** – In **Settings** > **Screen Time**, tap **Downtime** to schedule time away from the screen. You can pick a start and an end time during which you are either entirely or partially offline. You can also designate which apps should always be allowed.

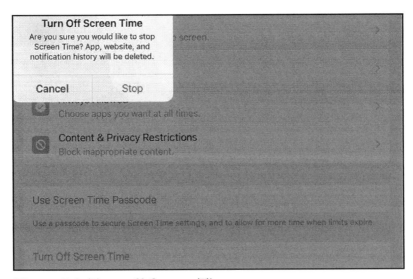

Figure 8.5: Turn off Screen Time

❑ **Set App Limits** – Tap **App Limits**, and then tap **Add Limit** to set regular time limits for app categories. Next, tap one or more categories, and tap **Add**. You can adjust the displayed timer to the amount of time you designate to use these apps. You can also delete past limits in this screen.

❑ **Always Allowed** – Tap **Always Allowed**, and then use the red minus signs or green plus signs to allow (or disallow) specific apps all the time.

❑ **Contact & Privacy Restrictions** – Tap this feature to block access to certain explicit sites, set age limits for movie viewing, and more. This is a helpful feature for parents to set up device restrictions for their kids. After enabling **Contact & Privacy Restrictions Settings** by moving the white circle to the right, you may be prompted to create a passcode which you can use thereafter to access or modify the limits you set up (for a minor). You can also tap **Set Up Screen Time for Family** to add a child, program further restrictions and also to receive weekly reports on usage by family members.

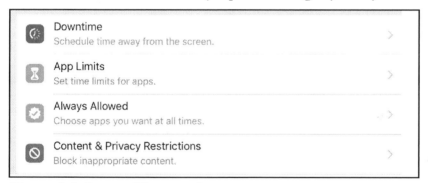

Figure 8.6: Screen Time settings

 Trick 88:

Turn Off the New Screen Time Feature

You may prefer to turn off the **Screen Time** feature and not have your screen time and app usage measured in such detail. Here's how to turn off **Screen Time**.

1. Tap **Settings**, and then tap **Screen Time**.

2. To turn off **Screen Time**, tap **Turn Off Screen Time**, and then tap **Stop**.

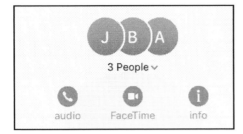

Figure 8.7: Start a FaceTime group call from iMessage

 Trick 89:

Start a Group Call Using FaceTime

Note: This feature may not be available in the iOS 12 initial release. It may be included in a future software iOS 12 update.

iOS 12 has added a wonderful feature that allows up to 32 people to participate in a video **FaceTime** call at the same time. You can start a group call using the **FaceTime** app or begin it from an existing group texting session. To keep track of who is speaking when more than one person is on a call, the video window of the current person that is speaking temporarily enlarges. O n certain iPhone models, you can also substitute character avatars such as **Animoji** instead of your own face (see the next trick). Here's how to start a group call using **FaceTime**.

1. Tap **FaceTime**, and then tap the **plus sign** at the top corner.

2. Tap the next **plus sign**, select contacts, then tap **Video** to start the call.

Note: You can also start a group call during an **iMessage** group chat by tapping the circles at the top of the chat (see Figure 8.7), and then tapping **FaceTime**.

Figure 8.8: Create a new Memoji in iMessage

Trick 90:

Create a Memoji (iPhone 10/X, XS/Max, XR, and newer-model iPhones only)

Animojis are emojis depicting characters (mostly animals) which serve as a personal symbol or avatar you can use in texting and elsewhere. **Animojis** in recent updates have introduced a ghost, koala, tiger, and Tyrannosaurus Rex. In addition, there is a new iOS 12 feature called a **Memoji**, which is a cartoon avatar that represents you – your skin color, hair style, head shape, and more. Here's how to create and work with your own personal **Memoji**.

1. From the **Home** screen, tap the **iMessage** texting app, and then tap the **Animoji** icon (monkey face) in the **App Drawer** below the text. (See Figure 8-8.)

2. Tap the **New Memoji** plus sign, and the follow the on-screen instructions to customize your **Memoji** with your skin color, freckles, hair color, eye color, head shape, nose size, and more.

3. Tap the **Done** icon to complete the process of creating your personal avatar.

To share your new **Memoji**, select the monkey icon after initiating a message. Note that you can stick out your tongue, make a face, or wink, and the animated **Memoji** will imitate it. You can tap the **Memoji** to add it into a message, or record a video clip of your **Memoji** complete with audio that lasts up to 30 seconds.

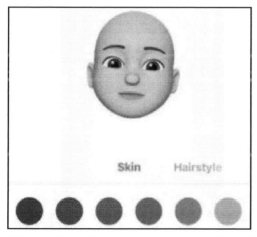

Figure 8.9: Create a new Memoji in iMessage

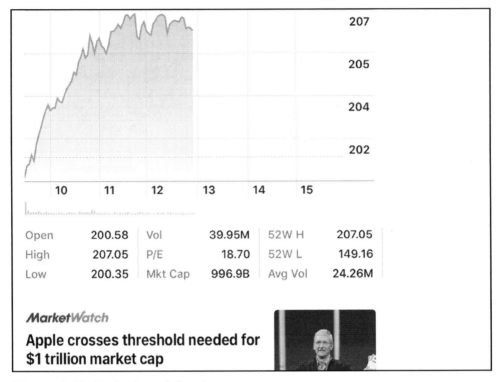

Figure 8.10: Redesigned Stocks app

 Trick 91:

Add a Stock to Your Watchlist in the Updated Stocks App

Apple has revamped the **Stocks** app, integrating it with up-to-the-minute news content, graphs, and more. You can use the search feature in the **Stocks** app to locate your own personal stocks, and you can add them to a customized watchlist.

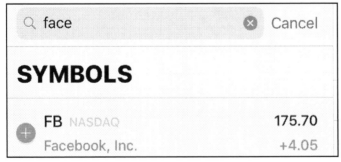

Figure 8.11: Add a stock to your watchlist

Figure 8.12: Menu icon

Here's how to customize your watchlist by adding your own personal stock holdings.

1. From the **Home** screen, tap the **Stocks** app, and then tap the menu icon at the bottom.

2. Tap the plus sign, then type the stock name in the search box that displays.

3. When the stock's name displays, tap the **green plus sign** at the left, and the stock will be added to your watchlist.

To delete a stock from your watchlist:

1. From the **Home** screen, tap the **Stocks** app, and then tap the menu icon at the bottom.

2. Tap the **red minus sign**, and the stock will be deleted from your watchlist.

To change the order of the stocks in your watchlist:

1. From the **Home** screen, tap the **Stocks** app, and then tap the menu icon at the bottom.

2. Press down on the **move** icon, and then drag the stock up or down in the list.

3. Release the stock's move icon, and then tap **Done** at the top.

Figure 8.13: The Move icon

Figure 8.14: Swipe down to bring up Control Center

 Trick 92

Use iPhone Gestures for your iPad

If your iPad has been updated to iOS 12, you may notice that you can use the same gestures that you use on your iPhone 10/X, XS/Max, and XR models. For instance, you can now swipe up from the bottom of the screen to bring back the **Home** screen on your iPad, instead of using the **Home** button to initiate this action. Here's how to access **Control Center**, using the iPad gestures.

1. From the **Home** screen, place your finger near the top right corner.

2. Swipe down to bring up **Control Center**. You can swipe back up when you are done using this app.

Trick 93:

Look Up Lyrics in Apple Music

The **Shazam** app identifies songs by their melodies, but Apple's **Music** app now lets you search for songs by typing in just a small sentence or phrase from any song. To search for songs by their lyrics, perform the following actions:

1. From the **Home** screen, tap the **Music** app, and then tap the **Search** box at the bottom right.

2. Tap the **Music** app, and then type some of the words of the lyrics into the search box. You may notice some suggestions as you type. Tap any recognizable results to see song titles that contain those lyrics.

Figure 8.15: Search by lyrics to locate a song in Apple Music

 ## Trick 94:

Close Running Apps on the iPhone 10/X

If you currently own an iPhone 10/X, but have also owned earlier models, you may have noticed that it took extra steps to close each app on the iPhone 10/X. Before iOS 12, you had to swipe up from the bottom to the middle of the screen and then hold to view the running apps. After that, you had to press on each app name to access a red minus sign. At that point, you could either tap the minus sign, or swipe up to close the running app. In iOS 12, you don't have to press each app to access the minus sign. Here's how to access and close running apps in iOS 12 on your iPhone.

1. From the **Home** screen, swipe up from the bottom to the middle of the screen and then hold to view running apps.

2. Swipe upwards on each app (or on two or three apps at once), just like on the most other iPhone models to close running apps. Note that on earlier iPhone models, you can close running apps by double-pressing the **Home** button and then swiping upwards.

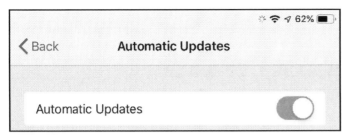

Figure 8.16: Turn on automatic updates

 Trick 95:

Turn On Automatic Software Updates

If you are tired of manually updating each iOS version as it comes along, you can turn on automatic updates. These updates will be installed automatically after they have been downloaded. A notification will display before the updates are installed. Here's how to turn on automatic software updates.

1. From the **Home** screen, tap **Settings**, and then tap **General**.

2. Tap **Software Update**, and then tap **Automatic Updates**.

3. Drag the white circle to the right to enable automatic updates.

Note: Your device must be charging and connected to Wi-Fi to complete the updating process.

Note: Many people prefer to wait a few weeks after new updates first come out in order to check if there are glitches that could affect their device. If you prefer to wait before updating, do not turn on automatic software updates. If you don't turn on automatic updates, you will see a red badge on your **Settings** app icon when updates are available. You can use the first few steps above to choose the time when you want to update.

 Trick 96:

Create a Shortcut in Siri

Siri Shortcuts is a new feature that allows you to group several commands together in a named shortcut, which can then be initiated by saying (or typing) the new name when accessing **Siri**. For instance, you can create a shortcut called "Ski Day" that causes **Siri** to carry out several actions such as to display a snow report, show current weather, deliver directions to your chosen ski slope in **Maps**, and more. Next, access **Siri** and say (or type) the

the name of the shortcut. You can access **suggested** shortcuts in **Settings** to start creating shortcuts right away, but you should also download the **Shortcuts** app from the **App Store** to create shortcuts (in **Library**) or access pre-fabricated shortcuts (in **Gallery**). You can also find shortcuts created by others by searching for **Siri Shortcuts** on the Web and then downloading each with a simple tap. You will then be prompted to add them to your **Shortcuts** app.

To access existing suggestions for shortcuts in the **Settings** app:

1. From the **Home** screen, tap **Settings**, and then tap **Siri & Search**.

2. Tap **All Shortcuts**, tap a suggested shortcut, tap the red record button, and then say a keyword that will initiate this shortcut in the future.

3. Tap **Done**, access **Siri**, and say (or type) the keyword to initiate the shortcut.

    Note: To create a shortcut in the **Shortcut** app, launch the app, tap **Library**, and tap **Create Shortcut**. You will be prompted with suggested shortcuts to create. You may prefer to start out instead by tapping **Gallery**, tapping one of the pre-existing shortcuts, tapping **Get Shortcut**, and then tapping **Done**. Downloaded shortcuts will also display in the **Gallery**.

 # Trick 97:

Record a Dictation with the Updated Voice Memos App

The **Voice Memos** app could be found in early iOS versions but it has been completely redesigned in iOS 12. Now in iOS 12, voice memos recorded on one device will be synced to iCloud so that they are available on all devices. Before you record in **Voice Memos**, you should go to **Settings** and make sure that you select the correct settings. For instance, if you are using voice memos to dictate personal notes, leave the quality setting to **Compressed**. If you are recording music or interviews, change the setting to **Lossless**, so it will record with higher quality. Here's how to create a voice memo.

1. From the **Home** screen, launch the **Voice Memos** app.

2. Tap the red **Record** button and begin to speak. Note that you can stop or pause the recording, and then continue if needed.

3. Tap **Done** to stop recording.

    You can edit, trim, delete, or share your voice memo with others.

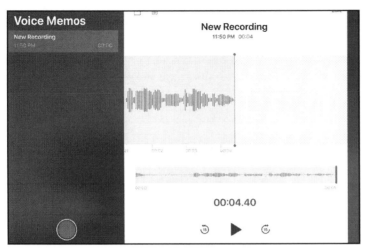

Figure 8.17: Voice memos

 Trick 98:

Create a Second Face ID (iPhone X models only)

If you wear prescription sunglasses, you will find that you have to remove them every time you want to unlock your phone using **Face ID**. Otherwise, you will have to enter your passcode over and over, which obviates the point of using **Face ID**. Another reason to create a second ID might be to allow a spouse or other person to be able to access your phone using your **Face ID**.

Now iOS 12 allows you to add a second **Face ID**. Using the **Face ID & Passcode** feature called **Set Up an Alternate Appearance,** you can enroll an alternate look, in addition to the one that accompanies your first **Face ID**. **Face ID** is similar to the extra fingerprint features used with **Touch ID**. Here's how to register a second face for **Face ID**!

1. From the **Home** screen, tap **Settings**, and then tap **Face ID & Passcode**.

2. Tap **Set Up an Alternative Appearance**, and then tap **Get Started**.

3. Follow the on-screen instructions and scan your second **Face ID**.

Note: Once you set up the alternate appearance, you can't delete it. However, you can add a second appearance to replace the old one by tapping the **Reset Face ID** button that displays and then re-scan to replace (delete) the former appearance.

Trick 99:

Change Siri's Voice to South African or Irish

In a small change introduced by iOS 12, **Siri** now can have an Irish or South African accent which adds to the existing American, Australian, and British accents. These new accents are available in both male and female versions. Here's how to change Siri's accent on your iPhone or iPad:

1. From the **Home** screen, tap **Settings**, and then tap **Siri & Search**.

2. Tap **Siri Voice (or Language)**, and then choose one of the accents for **Siri**.

‹ Siri & Search	**Language**
English (Canada)	
English (India)	
English (Ireland)	
English (New Zealand)	

Figure 8.18: Change Siri's accent

 ## Trick 100:

Use Waze & Google Maps with CarPlay

If you have a vehicle that supports **CarPlay**, you can now use it with third-party apps like **Waze** and **Google Maps** instead of just Apple **Maps** in iOS 12. Simply locate these apps on select models with **CarPlay**-powered dashboards.

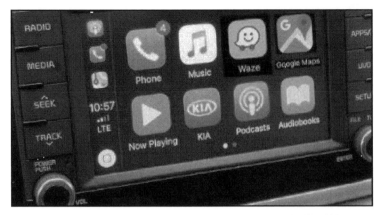

Figure 8.19: Use Waze & Google Maps with CarPlay

 Trick 101:

Use AirDrop to Transfer Passwords (& more)

In iOS 12, you can use the **AirDrop** feature (present on earlier versions for transferring photos, documents, etc.) to transfer **passwords** to another device. In the past, as long as your device was near to another device, you could transfer many photos and documents easily, without having to upload them or email/text them to another device. Now, in iOS 12, you can also share saved **passwords** between your own or another person's device (such as a family member or friend). First let's review how to transfer photos using **AirDrop**.

Note: To try this trick, use two devices (iPad/iPhone). You can also practice with another person who has an iPad/iPhone handy.

1. Swipe up from the bottom frame of your device (or swipe down from the upper right-hand corner of your iPad or iPhone 10/X, XS/Max, XR) to bring up **Control Center**.

2. Long-press the panel that shows **Airplane** mode, **Bluetooth**, and **Wireless** to access **AirDrop**, tap the **AirDrop** icon, and then tap **Everyone** (or **Contacts Only**).

3. Close **Control Center**, and then tap the **Photos** app.

4. Select a photo, and then tap the **Share** icon.

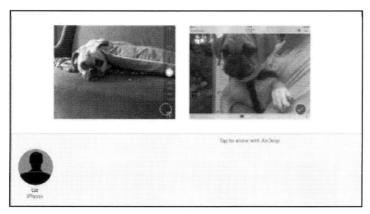

Figure 8.20: Use AirDrop to transfer a photo

5. Locate the other device. It will display at the top of the list of sharing possibilities.

6. Tap the other device name (see above illustration showing a person's head and name), and the picture will be transferred to that device.

Note: It is important to know that **AirDrop > Everyone** should be used only temporarily and then turned off afterwards, because otherwise it can open your device to strangers. If you are in a public place and want to exchange photos with a friend or member of your family, it is preferable to select **AirDrop > Contacts Only** (as long as they are a contact). For security reasons, after using **AirDrop**, you should turn it off. Here's how!

   To disable **AirDrop**:

1. Bring up **Control Center**.

2. **Long-press** the panel displaying **Airplane** mode, tap **AirDrop**, and then tap **Receiving Off**.

Figure 8.21: Use AirDrop to transfer a password

To transfer passwords between two devices:

Note: To try this trick, use two devices (iPad/iPhone). You can also practice with another person who has an iPad/iPhone handy.

1. Swipe up from the bottom frame of your device (or swipe down from the upper right-hand corner of your iPad or iPhone 10/XS/Max, or XR) to bring up **Control Center**.

2. **Long-press** the panel that contains **Airplane** mode, **Bluetooth**, and **Wireless**, tap **AirDrop**, and then tap **Everyone** (or **Contacts Only**).

3. Close **Control Center**, and then tap **Settings**.

4. Tap **Passwords & Accounts**, and then tap **Website & App Passwords**.

5. Tap one of the saved logins in the list (or if this area is empty, press the + sign to add a password that lets you log in to a website or to a program), **long-press** the password field, and then select the **AirDrop** option that displays. The password will be transferred to the other device.

Passcode, Touch ID, and Face ID Settings

Many people find it annoying to find their iPhone/iPad always signing off because this forces them to constantly sign in with a numeric passcode. However, having a passcode is one of the best ways to ensure privacy from identity theft and hackers who can get into emails, contacts, and more, and do a lot of damage. Having no passcode (or an easy-to-try 4-digit passcode like 1234) is like having no locks on your house door at night.

Set or Update Your Passcode ASAP

If you don't have a passcode, you should create one ASAP. If you have a 4-digit passcode, it is best to change it to a 6-digit passcode. Here's how!

1. Tap the **Settings** app on the **Home** screen.

2. Tap **Touch ID & Passcode (**or **Face ID & Passcode** on the iPhone 10/X, XS/Max, or XR).

Note: On devices without **Touch ID** or **Face ID**, go to **Settings** > **Passcode**.

3. If you already have a passcode set up, enter the passcode in the keypad that comes up. If you do not have a passcode, you can set one up in the **Passcode Lock** screen by tapping **Turn Passcode On**.

4. It is best to enter a 6-digit passcode. If you have an existing 4-digit passcode, add a 00 or 11 to it so you can remember it just as easily as the one you used before!

Figure A.1: Enter passcode screen

Change Auto-Lock Settings

You may notice that your iPhone/iPad goes to sleep every so often, and you have to continually plug in your passcode. Your device may be set to **Auto-Lock**, which lets you set a time for your device to lock when you aren't using it. For security reasons, it is suggested that you set the **auto-lock** feature to a shorter time to put your device to sleep when it's not being used.

It may be an inconvenience to enter your passcode so much, but it is the best safeguard to have the phone lock when it is not in use. Here's how to set your **auto-lock** timing!

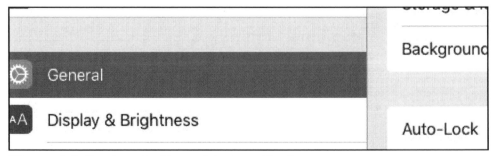

Figure A.2: Settings > General > Auto-Lock

Set Up Your Passcode & Touch ID   **115**

To change your **auto-lock** settings:

1. Tap the **Settings** app.

2. Tap **General**, and then tap **Auto-Lock**.

3. Pick one of the times listed.

Note: For security reasons, once again, it is best to pick the shortest time.

Set Up Your Touch ID

Before beginning, make sure that both the **Home** button and your finger are clean and dry. Then perform the following actions:

1. Tap **Settings**, **Touch ID & Passcode,** then enter your passcode.

2. Tap **Add a Fingerprint.**

3. As directed, touch the **Home** button with your finger lightly. Hold it there until you until you're asked to lift your finger.

Apple advises you to lift and rest your finger slowly, making small adjustments to the position of your finger each time as directed. The next screen will ask you to adjust your grip. Hold your device as you normally would when unlocking it, and touch the **Home** button with the outer areas of your fingertip, instead of the center area. You will be notified when it is complete. Thereafter, you can just press your finger to the Home button to unlock your device.

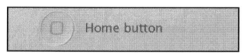

Figure A.3: Home button Touch ID

Set Up Your Face ID

Before beginning, make sure that there isn't anything covering the camera or your face. According to Apple, **Face ID** is designed to work with glasses or contacts. Then perform the following actions:

1. Tap **Settings**, then tap **Face ID & Passcode**.

2. Enter your passcode if prompted, otherwise go to the next step.

3. Tap **Set Up Face ID**, then move your face in front of your device and tap **Get Started**.

4. Look directly into your iPhone and place your face inside the frame. Gently move your head to complete the circle.

Note: If you're unable to move your head, tap **Accessibility Options**.

5. When you finish the first **Face ID** scan, tap **Continue**. Move your head again to complete the circle.

6. A message will appear, informing you that **Face ID** setup is complete. Tap **Done** to complete the process.

Note: You can set up a second **Face ID** assignment on your iPhone or iPad, either for an alternate look (e.g. prescription sunglasses) or for another person. For more information, see **Chapter 8**.

Note: If you didn't set a passcode, you need to create one to function as an alternative way to verify your identity. See the earlier section in this appendix for the steps to set up a passcode.

Other Courses from iWorkshopAcademy.com

- ❒ **100+ iPhone/iPad Tricks You Can Do Right Now (iOS 12)** - The complete online course with individual lessons, outline, and handouts for each class module.

- ❒ **Learn iPhone/iPad 101** - A complete iPhone/iPad basic and self-paced online course with individual lessons, outline, and handouts for each class module.

- ❒ **Learn iPhone/iPad 102** - A complete iPhone/iPad Intermediate and self-paced online course with individual lessons, outline, and handouts for each class module.

- ❒ **Camera and Photo iPhone/iPad Essential Tricks to Know** - Take better pictures! A complete, self-paced online course with individual lessons, outline, and handouts for each class module.

- ❒ **Introduction to Social Media: Facebook, Twitter, Instagram, and Pinterest** - A complete, self-paced, online course with individual lessons, outline, and handouts for each class module.

- ❒ **Harnessing the Power of Safari: Safe Browsing, Online Shopping, and More** - A complete and self-paced online course with individual lessons, outline, and handouts for each class module.

❑   **Learn iPhone/iPad Essential Apps** - A complete and self-paced online course with individual lessons, outline, and handouts for each class module.

❑   **Travel Smart** - A complete, self-paced online course with individual lessons, outline, and handouts for each class module.

For more information, see iworkshopacademy.com/courses.

iPhone Shortcuts

This appendix can be used as a quick reference for actions you can use on the iPhone 10/X, XS/Max, XR or earlier devices.

Task	iPhone 10/X, XS/Max, XR	iPhone 8/8 Plus & Earlier Models (6, 6S, 7)
Wake Up Device	Tap Screen	Press Home Button
Return to Home Screen	Swipe Up From Base	Press Home Button
Clear Out Running Apps	Swipe Up from Base, Stop Midway & Hold, & then Swipe Up	Double-Click Home & Swipe Up
Take a Screenshot	Press On/Off & Volume Up Buttons at the Same Time	Press On/Off & Home Buttons at the Same Time
Launch Siri	Press & Hold On/Off Button	Press & Hold Home Button
Launch Emergency Service (if set up)	Press the On/Off Button 5 Times Rapidly	Press the On/Off Button 5 Times Rapidly
Access Camera from Lock Screen	Swipe Left on the Lock Screen or Tap the Camera icon	Swipe Left on the Lock Screen or Tap the Camera icon
Turn Device Off	Hold Down On/Off Button and Volume Up Button at the Same Time	Hold Down On/Off Button and Home Button at the Same Time

Glossary

Lingo to Know

Below is a small glossary of terms that are used in this guide, along with their definitions.

App - The term "app" is a shortened version of "application". In the world of technology, an application is a specialized software program. For example, a spreadsheet program like Microsoft Excel can be called an application, because it is a software program that allows you to calculate numbers and create spreadsheets. An "app" is actually a shortened version of a software application and it is often even more specialized. For instance, you could download a calculator app to calculate, a tipping app to use at restaurants, and other numeric-oriented programs from the **App** store, and each has its own specific focus. Note that Apple calls all of its programs "apps", and that apps appear as icons on your **Home** screen, (e.g. the familiar **Camera**, **Photos**, **Contacts**, and **Settings** apps.)

Home screen - The **Home** screen is the main screen that displays all of your apps as little icons.

iOS - The letters "OS" stand for "operating system." An operating system is the main software that takes care of all the underlying processes that operate your iPhone/iPad and/or computer. A typical operating system allows you to communicate with your device without having to learn complex computer commands. Examples of operating systems include Windows, Android, and Linux. A version number is given to all new updates of any operating system (e.g. iOS 12); however, smaller updates (mostly fixes) are often added after a major update (e.g. iOS 12.1.2). Apple always puts a small "i" in front of its products, and its operating system is no exception. This is why it is called iOS! When you are prompted to update your software in the **Settings** app under the **General** selection, the system will check if you have the latest version, prompt you to download, and allow you to install the newest version, if available.

Lock screen - The **Lock** screen is the first screen you encounter when you press the **Home** button on your device. It has to be unlocked by your face, your fingerprint or by typing in a passcode (the numbers you type in in order to access the **Home** screen) depending on the model of your device.

Notifications - You receive notifications all the time on your device from such apps as **Phone** (showing missed calls), **iMessage** (showing missed texts), **Calendar** (showing upcoming events), and more. Notifications display in different ways on your device, such as sounds, badges (the red numbered circles that display on an app icon), banners (messages showing at the top of the screen), and more. You can find notifications gathered together in the **Notifications Center**, which displays when you swipe down from the top frame of the iP hone or iPad from any screen. To respond to a notification, swipe left over it, and then tap **respond**. To open an app to respond, swipe right over the notification.

Passcode screen - The **Passcode** screen is the screen that is accessed when you press the **Home** button from the **Lock** screen. The **Passcode** screen is where you type the 4-digit or 6-digit numbers that take you to the **Home** screen.

Widget - A widget is a very small, specialized software program that can be thought of as a limited piece of an app, or a mini app. For instance, Apple's weather widget displays updated weather on your **Lock** screen. It is very helpful to get the latest temperature information, and the weather widget draws its updates from Apple's **Weather** app. However, Apple's full **Weather** app, when launched by tapping the **Weather** icon, supplies much more weather information on more than one screen.

Index

Page numbers followed by an *f* indicate figures. Numbers followed by a *g* indicate glossary items.

Made in the USA
Lexington, KY
18 August 2019